# Database Benchmarking
### Practical Methods for Oracle & SQL Ser

*IT In-Focus Series*

MW00487733

*Dr. Bert Scalzo*
*Donald K. Burleson*
*Claudia Fernandez*
*Kevin Klein*
*Mike Ault*

RAMPANT
TECHPRESS

*I dedicate this book to Christian Hasker and David Pearson for their input in the database best practices methodology; to Billy Bosworth for his mentoring and support; to the Benchmark Factory development team, Kevin Dalton, Tracey Ashwell, Bernard Farrell and Nitesh Mohanlal for building such an amazing tool.*

~Claudia Fernandez

*I dedicate this book to my new grandson, Michael Caleb Bojczuk with all my love and to my daughter Michelle and her husband Michael.*

~Mike Ault

*I dedicate this book to Noel Burleson.*

~Don Burleson

*To my dog Max - my best friend in the whole world!*

~Bert Scalzo, PhD

*This work is dedicated to Dylan, Emily, Anna Lynn, and Katie Jo. You, my beloved children, are the wellspring for all my joys.*

~Kevin Klin

# Database Benchmarking
## Practical Methods for Oracle & SQL Server

By Mike Ault, Donald K. Burleson, Claudia Fernandez, Kevin Klein, & Dr Bert Scalzo

Copyright © 2006 by Rampant TechPress. All rights reserved.
Printed in the United States of America.
Published in Kittrell, North Carolina, USA.

**IT In-Focus Series:** Book 3
**Series Editor:** Donald K. Burleson
**Editors:** Janet Burleson, Robin Haden, & Cindy Cairns
**Production Editor:** Teri Wade
**Cover Design:** Janet Burleson
**Illustrations:** Mike Reed
**Printing History:** September 2006 for First Edition

ISBN: 0-9776715-3-4
Library of Congress Control Number: 2006931339

# Table of Contents

# Using the Online Code Depot

Purchase of this book provides complete access to the online code depot that contains the sample code scripts. All of the code depot scripts in this book are located at the following URL:

www.rampant.cc/benchmark.htm

All of the code scripts in this book are available for download in zip format, ready to load and use. If technical assistance is needed with downloading or accessing the scripts, please contact Rampant TechPress at info@rampant.cc.

Your purchase also includes a free evaluation copy of Quest solutions to help you develop, diagnose, validate and optimize your database and its code.

The Quest Software Database Tuning Methodology encompasses Quest **Benchmark Factory® for Databases, Toad™ Xpert** and **Spotlight®**. No matter which database platform you are running, Quest Software ensures optimal performance and scalability.

For more information or to download, visit:

**Benchmark Factory for Databases**
**http://www.quest.com/benchmark_factory/default.aspx**
**Download Toad Xpert**
**http://www.quest.com/toad/**
**Download Spotlight**
**http://www.quest.com/spotlight/**

## Supplemental Materials

Your purchase of this book entitles you to receive free evaluation copies of these benchmarking tools:

- Diagnose performance issues with Quest *Spotlight®*

- Develop and optimize code with *Toad™ Xpert*

- Validate the scalability of your database environment with *Benchmark Factory® for Databases*


For more information or to download, visit:

**Benchmark Factory for Databases**
**http://www.quest.com/benchmark_factory/default.aspx**

**Download ToadXpert**
**http://www.quest.com/toad/**

**Download Spotlight**
**http://www.quest.com/spotlight/**

# Conventions Used in this Book

It is critical for any technical publication to follow rigorous standards and employ consistent punctuation conventions to make the text easy to read. However, this is not an easy task. Within database terminology there are many types of notation that can confuse a reader. For example, some Oracle utilities such as STATSPACK and TKPROF are always spelled in CAPITAL letters, while Oracle parameters and procedures have varying naming conventions in the database documentation. It is also important to remember that many database commands are case sensitive, and are always left in their original executable form, and never altered with italics or capitalization.

Hence, all Rampant TechPress books follow these conventions:

**Parameters** - All database parameters will be *lowercase italics*. Exceptions to this rule are parameter arguments that are commonly capitalized (KEEP pool, TKPROF); these will be left in ALL CAPS.

**Variables** – All procedural language (e.g. PL/SQL) program variables and arguments will also remain in *lowercase italics* (*dbms_job*, *dbms_utility*).

**Tables & Dictionary Objects** – All data dictionary objects are referenced in lowercase italics (*dba_indexes*, *v$sql*). This includes all *v$* and *x$* views (*x$kcbcbh*, *v$parameter*) and dictionary views (*dba_tables*, *user_indexes*).

**SQL** – All SQL is formatted for easy use in the code depot, and all SQL is displayed in lowercase. The main SQL terms (select, from, where, group by, order by, having) will always appear on a separate line.

**Programs & Products** – All products and programs that are known to the author are capitalized according to the vendor specifications (IBM, Benchmark Factory, etc). All names known by Rampant TechPress to be trademark names appear in this text as initial caps. References to UNIX are always made in uppercase.

# Acknowledgements

This type of highly technical reference book requires the dedicated efforts of many people. Though we are the authors, our work ends when we deliver the content. After each chapter is delivered, several Oracle & SQL Server professionals carefully review and correct the technical content. After completion of the technical review, experienced copy editors polish the grammar and syntax.

The finished work is then reviewed as page proofs and turned over to the production manager, who arranges the creation of the online code depot and manages the cover art, printing distribution, and warehousing.

In short, the authors play a small role in the development of this book, and we need to thank and acknowledge everyone who helped bring this book to fruition:

**Janet Burleson**, for the production management, including the coordination of the cover art, page proofing, printing, and distribution.

**Teri Wade**, for her help in the production of the page proofs.

**Robin Haden**, for helping edit the page proofs.

**Mike Reed**, for his exceptional illustrations.

**John Lavender**, for his assistance with the web site, creating the code depot and the online shopping cart for this book.

With our sincerest thanks,

*Don Burleson, Claudia Fernandez,*
*Mike Ault, Kevin Klein, &Dr Bert Scalzo*

# Preface

Predicting the future behavior of a database has always been fraught with danger. It is challenging to derive a benchmark study that accurately reflects the real-world processing demands of a complex database, especially when it has tens of thousands of end users, hundreds of transactions per second and a Service Level Agreement (SLA) that mandates a sub-second response time.

Those who forget the past are condemned to repeat it.

*George Santanaya*

Database professionals have struggled for decades with deriving predictive models for the behavior of their systems.

Simulating the activities of a large number of end users is a giant challenge, but there are some important tips and tools used by benchmarking professionals to ensure the development of a statistically legitimate model that will predict actual user loads.

This book is the result of many years of experience in benchmarking real databases. We strive to provide you with a solid foundation into the tools and techniques for developing and executing statistically valid tests.

# Introduction to Benchmarking

**The trend is clear!**

Tomorrow we will see
lightly-scattered I/O
bottlenecks clearing
into afternoon
latch contention.

## Database Predictive Analysis

For the IT manager charged with predicting database performance, benchmark predictions present a huge challenge. It is very difficult to use benchmarks to prove that an artificial load is representative of real-world processing conditions, yet the IT manager is bound by strict Service Level Agreements (SLA) whereby they must guarantee response time and database throughput. However, with a basic understanding of statistics and regression techniques, any IT manager can conduct a valid benchmark that predicts scale-related slowdowns.

Many database vendors are recognizing the value of predictive analytics, and companies such as Oracle have invested millions of dollars into tools that can predict when an object needs to be reorganized and when general database administration is required.

## Database Benchmark Validity

In the realm of database performance analytics, there is no substitute for a benchmark test that closely parallels real-world processing conditions. However, it may be impossible to hire 10,000 end users to simulate the activities of an active end user community, yet database professionals are required to provide statistically valid predictions about the performance of their databases under high load conditions.

There has been a backlash against test case scenarios where a small and inconsequential test is extrapolated to a larger system. Today's database professionals recognize that there is no shortcut for a performance simulation that closely resembles real-world processing. As user load increases, data concurrency issues arise and database professionals must be able to forecast bottlenecks that arise as a function of high user activity.

There are other tools available to measure database performance in real-time, most notably the Quest SQL Optimizer tool. This tool offers a non-intrusive database object and source code scanner that identifies possible performance problems offline or online, enabling the DBA to be proactive in troubleshooting bottlenecks before they arise. Quest SQL Optimizer also includes a predictive "what if" function that analyzes the impact of potential database changes before they are implemented ensuring that expected performance gains are realized.

Vendors continue to collect time-series data for performance forecasting but they fall far short of a valid database benchmark. For example, in Oracle Enterprise Manager the software collects baseline metrics and statistically characterizes specific system metrics over time periods matched to system usage patterns. These statistical profiles of expected metric behavior are used to implement adaptive alert thresholds that can signal administrators when statistically unusual metric events occur.

## The Problems of Adaptive Threshold Forecasting

Assuming that database systems are normally stable and performance problems rare, it is reasonable to expect that actual performance events will be highly correlated with observed unusual values in some metric or other. Therefore, it is hoped that baseline driven adaptive thresholds will both reduce configuration overhead for administrators and more reliably signal real problems than fixed alert thresholds.

Today, database predictive analytics are concerned with predicting individual database events rather than forecasting the holistic behavior of performance. For example, the Oracle Automated Workload Repository (AWR) provides data for common database predictions such as:

- Predicting the reduction in disk space, logical I/O and physical I/O from reorganizing a table or index.

- Using linear regression techniques to predict a future time when the database will exhaust server resources such as RAM or CPU.

Unfortunately, these pseudo-benchmarks will only alert the database professionals after the database has experienced a serious bottleneck condition, but what is needed is a method that will accurately predict the stress load where response time will decline.

The following section will provide a quick overview of predictive analytics in the real world and show how they apply to database benchmarks.

## Predictive Modeling in the Real-world

Traditional Data Mining and Data Warehouse tools have utilities for identifying significant correlations (i.e. consumer buying patterns). The predictive probability is more important than the reason for the correlation. For example, if there is a 70% chance that people who bought *Waldo's Widgets* will also buy *Cobb's Cogs*, that is all the information needed to launch a marketing campaign targeting consumers of *Waldo's Widgets*.

The causation of a correlation is not as important as the strength of the correlation itself. There are many natural events in the world that show a high correlation, and periodicals such as *Poor Richards Almanac* served as a reporting vehicle for predictive modeling in past centuries. The following are several examples of such correlations and predictive models:

- **Tour Operators:** Seafaring folks know that the photoluminescent ritual of the Ocean Glowworm breeding always occurs on the 4th and 5th nights after a full moon. The cause of this behavior may be interesting, but all the tour operators need to know is that there is a 90% probability that their tour boat guests will observe acres of luminescent glowworms on these special nights.

- **Farmers:** Farmers have known for centuries that root crops, such as potatoes, turnips, should always be planted right after the full moon and always before the new moon to achieve optimal growth. The causation is fascinating, of course, but the real value is the strong correlation of crop yield with lunar cycles.

- **Marketers:** In today's point-of-sale (POS) Oracle data warehouses perform multivariate chi-square analysis to categorize groups of consumers and predict their propensity for buying a certain type of product. Product manufacturers spend hundreds of millions of dollars a year on advertising. Being able to target their messages to those with a higher probability to buy the product can save them millions of misdirected advertising dollars each year.

- **Psychologists:** In personality testing, such as the Minnesota Multiphasic Personality Inventory (MMPI)test, a database of millions of respondents has been created and surprising correlations have been found. For example, the true/false answer to the statement "*I prefer a bath to a shower*" has a very high correlation to the MMPI scale. To date, no psychological researchers have discovered why people with a low self concept prefer different bathing techniques, but that does not diminish this question's value in personality assessment.

For databases, common predictive applications are common and one does not have to look far to see the application of database predictive modeling:

- **Amazon Book Suggestions:** Once a selection of interest to the reader is made on the Amazon website, a notice to the effect of "People who bought this book also enjoyed this book" will appear.

- **IBM's Predictive Failure Analysis (PFA):** This is a tool used to predict server failures and increases uptime by allowing the database professional to receive proactive alerts as much as 24-48 hours in advance of failures.

- **Targeted Advertising:** Data warehouses spend millions of dollars analyzing buying patterns to determine the probability that a consumer will be interested in a specific product.

- **Personality Tests:** The MMPI is used to assess personality and predict predispositions to behavior disorders. There are a number of industries that use the results of this test to identify and eliminate potential security threats.

In sum, predictive modeling exists in the world of probabilities, and it is the strength of the correlation itself that has value. While the causation behind the correlation may be interesting, the cold, hard numbers drive management decisions.

# Benefit of Predictive Analysis

The vast majority of database systems have repeating patterns and trends. Finding these trends and exceptions helps database professionals initially in identifying tuning opportunities such as sub-optimal SQL and system bottlenecks. Once the application, SQL and objects, such as tables and indexes, are optimized, the database must still be monitored to spot times when database resources must be reallocated. Examples of the types of database systems that have repeating patterns of usage include:

- **Financial Systems:** End users have well-defined hours of work, and batch jobs are routinely scheduled for financial rollups and book closing.

- **Manufacturing Systems:** The processing steps for a product from raw materials to finished product are nearly completely predictable.

- **Business Management Systems:** Oracle systems that are used for standard business functions like human resources, accounting, order tracking tend to have well-defined usage patterns and regularly scheduled reporting.

Of course, not every database system will have repeating patterns of usage, and such systems may not benefit from a predictive approach:

- **Ad-hoc Query Databases:** Read-only databases that are created for end user query may not have any identifiable trends of usage. Examples would include data warehouse query database for Business Objects and Crystal reports.

- **Laboratory Information Management Databases(LIMS):** LIMS databases will load and analyze data on an ad hoc basis.

- **Scientific Research Databases:** Oracle systems that crunch data from experiments are notoriously devoid of repeating patterns and trends.

It is important to remember that almost all databases have scheduled tasks, both for the end user and the DBA. The following section will show how benchmark performance metrics can be used to predict future database performance.

At this point it should be clear that database benchmarks must closely replicate real-world processing loads and that there is no substitute for a benchmark that has a high degree of predictive validity. It might be helpful to take a look at the TPC standards for database benchmarking.

## The Transaction Processing Performance Council

In an effort to standardize database benchmarks the Transaction Performance Processing Council (www.tpc.org) was founded. The TPC benchmarks are divided into four categories depending upon the characteristics of the back-end database. The categories are: TPC-C; TPC-H; TPC-R; and TPC-W.

The most common database benchmarks are the TPC-C for online transaction processing systems and TPC-H for decision support systems, but the real challenge is deriving the predictive capability of the benchmark tests.

## Benchmarking Bi-modal Databases

Databases generally have a distinct processing signature, which is modeled by hour of the day or day of the week; these processing signatures exist for disk I/O, CPU consumption, data buffer behavior, and shared pool activity. Essentially, these signatures can be combined to define specific modes of processing that are clearly identifiable and attributable to specific application requirements.

For example, a system could be operating in the online transaction processing (OLTP) mode during the day and then switch to data warehouse and decision support modes each evening.

It is foreseeable that databases will eventually be able to incorporate artificial intelligence to create a true self-tuning database. However, no one should underestimate the challenge and complexity of creating a self-tuning database engine. Large commercial databases have hundreds of parameters that interact with each other in a factorial fashion resulting in literally many billions of unique processing scenarios.

# Capacity Planning & Testing

Many shops are reluctant to devote the resources required to perform a legitimate real-world benchmark. Later chapters will cover information on how database benchmarking requires using the production server and a complex diagnostic and benchmark monitoring plan. Due to the inherent expense, many shops forgo a statistically valid benchmark, but savvy IT managers know that there are no shortcuts and a valid performance benchmark will be resource intensive.

The following generalities apply to database benchmarking:

- In a complex database, it is impossible to model every type of database load.

- The more specific the benchmark, the more limited are its predictive capabilities.

## Forecasting the Future

One confounding problem with any database benchmark is deriving a valid model that predicts scale-related bottlenecks and reliably identifies the point at which database response time degrades.

This issue of forecasting is not unique to database benchmarking and forecasting future behavior requires careful planning.

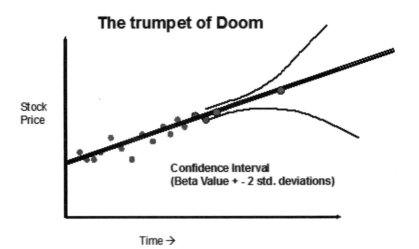

**Figure 1.1:** *The Trumpet of Doom*

Figure 1.1 shows that extrapolating a value far into the future reduces the confidence in the estimate. This is called "The trumpet of Doom" because the confidence interval, as measured by two standard deviations from the mean, widens dramatically as our estimates lengthen.

## Database Benchmarking Myths

There are many approaches to forecasting future database performance, but no database benchmark is perfect and the best that database professionals can hope for is a benchmark that provides a statistically reliable correlation between performance and scale. The following common myths can be seen in database benchmarking:

- All precepts or assumption must be valid; else the whole model is flawed.

- If an exception to a rule of thumb is found, the rule is worthless.

The goal of any database benchmark is to scan the benchmark data and identify statistically significant correlations within two standard deviations of the mean value, which allows predictions to be based on empirical samples rather than theory.

## Learning from Database Benchmarks

Database and hardware vendors have a high incentive to make their products perform fast, and they invest millions of dollars in optimizing their database benchmark tests.

The database professional can learn a great deal about how to optimize their server and database by reading the published benchmarks at www.tpc.org.

For example, TCP reveals details on hidden database parameters for an Oracle database:

```
_in_memory_undo=false
_cursor_cache_frame_bind_memory = true
_db_cache_pre_warm = false
_in_memory_undo=false
_check_block_after_checksum = false
_lm_file_affinity
```

# Conclusion

This chapter has introduced the basics of database benchmarking and predictive analysis for database performance. The main points of this chapter include:

- Today's IT managers must guarantee database performance with specific Service Level Agreements and must be able to forecast future database performance.

- It is impossible to prove future database performance and the best that database professionals can do is create a statistically valid correlation between scale and response time.

- There is no substitute for a real-world benchmark that directly simulates high volumes of common database transactions. Small scale test case scripts have no predictive validity.

Now, it is time to move on and examine database benchmarking standards and look at TPC-C, TCP-H, and the AS3AP model for database benchmarking.

# Database Benchmarks

*Benchmarking and measuring behavior under different stress levels; even nice databases can go bad.*

## Database Benchmarking

Database professionals juggle many challenges such as finding database breaking points, weak lines, and performance bottlenecks; determining database system throughput or capacity;

finding time or resources to test the database; optimizing systems configurations to meet customer's needs; keeping the database tuned; and managing platform changes.

Database administrators are typically responsible for implementing new platforms and maintaining the performance of existing platforms. New platform requirements come in such as: in the Oracle environment, implementing Real Application Clusters; or in SQL Server, moving from SQL Server 2000 to SQL Server 2005. These are examples of major platform changes that can affect performance and scalability of a database. Additionally, database professionals are required to evaluate new technologies and platforms such as different types of servers or to evaluate how different hardware resources such as CPUs, storage, and memory impact database performance and scalability.

Database professionals need to implement database testing and benchmarking practices to help them plan platform changes, minimize impact on production databases by testing before rolling-out system changes, and validate performance tuning efforts.

Database benchmarking offers repeatable, predictable and measurable results that can be used to perform an *apples-to-apples* comparison between different platforms, databases, and system configurations. A database benchmark provides the ability to compare database throughput between different states, such as before and after tuning configurations, before and after database migrations and upgrades, or between different hardware platforms.

The database benchmarking process utilizes software to test and compare computer hardware or software and implies that the software is used instead of actual users. Database benchmarking

---

involves the simulation of database sessions and execution of database transactions.

A benchmark is a test, or set of tests, that measures the performance of a system or subsystem while performing well-defined tasks. Frequently, benchmarks describe an industry standard ruler for comparing computer systems. The benchmark must measure system peak performance when performing typical operations within a problem area. Benchmarks measure the capacity of a system, often referred to as capacity planning and the performance of a particular application, such as a database.

## Standard Benchmarks

All good benchmarks use a well-defined testing methodology based on real-world use of a computer system. Benchmarks measure system performance in an accurate and reproducible manner, allowing IT professionals to properly judge the performance and capacity of a system-under-test.

The *Transaction Performance Processing Council* (www.tpc.org) is an organization, with representation from top hardware and software vendors, founded to define transaction processing and database benchmarks. TPC provides specifications on how benchmarks should be run and results reported.

In the mid-1980's computer system vendors and database vendors wanted to measure and prove which computer system was better. They began to make performance claims based upon IBM's TP1 benchmark that was designed to measure the performance of a system running ATM transactions in a batch mode. TPC started by formalizing the TP1 benchmark. In 1985 Jim Gray published the article "A Measure of Transaction Processing Power" which outlines a benchmark test for an on-line transaction processing named *DebitCredit*. Vendors utilized the TP1 and DebitCredit benchmarks using their own interpretation without any regulations until 1988 when TPC was founded.

TPC formalized the DebitCredit and TP1 benchmarks and evolved them into the TPC-A and TPC-B benchmarks respectively. In the early-90's, TPC defined the next evolution of database benchmarks, TPC-C for on-line transaction processing and TPC-D for decision support systems. The TPC-C is one of the most popular database benchmarks in the industry. TPC-D is replaced by the TPC-H benchmark which is also widely adopted in the industry. The TPC-E is the latest benchmark for on-line transaction processing that simulates the workload of a brokerage firm. TPC-C, TPC-H and TPC-E will be discussed in greater detail later in this chapter.

There are other well-known benchmarks which are not regulated by TPC. One of these benchmarks is the *Wisconsin*, invented by the University of Wisconsin. This benchmark is used to test the performance of relation query systems and puts to the limits the different components of a database system. For this reason, in the early-80's the Wisconsin benchmark became very popular with database vendors since it exposed weaknesses on the database systems that the vendors worked on improving.

The Wisconsin benchmark became the de-facto standard when it was released. It was used to compare different database vendors, however this benchmark was not designed to compare different database architectures and provide a true apples-to-apples comparison between different relational database systems. This was the motivation for the creation of the ANSI SQL Standard Scalable and Portable (AS3AP) benchmark. This benchmark is discussed in more detail later in this chapter.

# Benchmark Components

Benchmarks are formed by the following basic components:

- Specifications
- Control Logic
- Implementation

## Specifications

Benchmark specification documentation provides the following information:

- Details
- Design Goals
- Data Points
- Test Plan

### Details

Benchmarking details define metric objectives. The TPC disseminates objective, verifiable performance specifications to the IT industry. For example, the TPC-C specification defines the benchmarking process for on-line transaction processing.

### Design Goals

Well-defined design goals are essential for benchmark success. A benchmark should have the following characteristics:

- Scalability - Benchmarks, like enterprise systems, must be able to serve large numbers of users in a testing process without requiring major changes. During the execution of the benchmark, database users are simulated instead of having physical users running the database transactions. A good benchmarking system should offer scalability for running the benchmark transactions by a large number of simulated users, typically thousands.

- Easy-to-use and understand - Benchmarks should be simple to understand. A benchmarking system should be easy to install, run, and understand.

- Representative of the workload being tested - The workload being tested must accurately represent a system-under-test. For example, if a system-under-test is a database, the workload must reflect valid test data measurements, improved customer database access time, and other factors important to the overall operation of a database.

- Accuracy - Benchmark testing must accurately reflect the demands placed on enterprise systems. During the day-to-day operations of a database system, peak demands can quickly overload a system, causing customer dissatisfaction and profit loss. Benchmark testing accurately defines those demands avoiding profit-robbing system overloads.

## Data Points

Data points are the result of a benchmarking test. They represent the summary of the specified results for a user load. Data points provide the nuts and bolts information required to make accurate decisions on the performance capability of a system-under-test. An example of a data point is average transactions per second (TPS) at 200 users. Data points must be defined before implementing the benchmark testing process.

## Test Plan

All testing processes require a well-designed plan. This ensures real-world environments are duplicated during a benchmarking process.

## Control Logic

Control logic in the benchmarking process must have a well-defined initialization sequence that is separate from test and data collection. Control logic is not part of the benchmark. However, a benchmark does depend on the control logic for the following:

- Repeatability
- Accurate Statistics

### Repeatability

Repeatability represents benchmark results from multiple runs of the same test with consistent configuration test environments and parameters. If a benchmark is not sufficiently repeatable, the results have no meaning.

### Accurate Statistics

Accurate statistics are essential during a benchmarking process. Test result data, for example Transactions per Second (TPS), provides a user with the data necessary to determine where bottlenecks or potential enterprise problems may occur.

# Using Benchmark Factory

Quest Software's Benchmark Factory® allows the database professional to implement benchmark specifications and control logic. Benchmark Factory is an easy-to-use database performance and scalability testing that simulates users and transactions on the database and replays production workload in non-production environments. This enables the administrator to validate database scalability as user loads increase, application changes are made, and platform changes are implemented. Benchmark Factory supports Oracle, SQL Server, DB2, Sybase, MySQL, and other databases via ODBC connectivity.

Benchmark Factory enables the database professional to simulate real database application workloads using out-of-the-box industry standard benchmarks such as TPC-B, TPC-C, TPC-D, TPC-H, AS3AP and Scalable Hardware, to evaluate database scalability, test hardware/configurations, and determine system throughput.

With a simple wizard an industry standard benchmark can be created against a database. Besides simulating transactions from industry standard benchmarks, with Benchmark Factory the administrator can replay the production workload from Oracle and SQL Server traces, create customized user and transaction SQL scenarios, test SQL and database code (PL/SQL, T-SQL) for scalability, and validate scalability of Oracle Real-Application Clusters with built-in test workloads. Benchmark Factory measures and reports the test results and allows comparisons between different tests runs. Figure 2.1 shows the New Script wizard in Benchmark Factory where an administrator can select for each supported database the type of workload to generate.

**Figure 2.1:** `Benchmark Factory's New Script wizard allows you to select different types of workloads and test scenarios.`

The Industry standard benchmark option in Benchmark Factory's New Script wizard allows you to select from a variety of industry standard benchmarks implemented according to industry specifications. Figure 2.2 shows the industry standard benchmarks available in Benchmark Factory for Databases version 5.0.

**Figure 2.2:** *Benchmark Factory offers out-of-the-box Industry Standard Benchmarks.*

## TPC-C

The TPC-C benchmark for on-line transaction processing (OLTP) was introduced in 1992 by TPC. When TPC-C was released there were two other OLTP benchmarks adopted by the industry, TPC-A and TPC-B. The industry started to adopt TPC-C, and it became the de-facto standard for OLTP benchmarking replacing TPC-A and TPC-B.

TPC-C has its fundamentals in the TPC-A benchmark, which is the evolution of Gray's DebitCredit benchmark.

TPC-C simulates an order-entry application with users executing five different transactions against the database such as entering and delivering orders, recording payments, checking levels of stock at the warehouse and monitoring status of orders. These transactions are a combination of read-only and update-intensive transactions, so even the practical implementation of TPC-C is around an order processing system. TPC-C can be used to simulate the activities of complex OLTP enterprise environments.

The TPC-C benchmark simulates a wholesale supplier system with the following characteristics:

- Formed by a number of geographically distributed sales districts and warehouses.

- Each regional warehouse covers 10 districts.

- Each district servers 3,000 customers.

- Warehouses maintain a stock level for the 100,000 items available for sale.

- Customers place new orders or request status of existing orders.

- Orders have an average of 10 line items.

- 1% of all order lines are for items not available in stock at the regions warehouse, so it must be supplied by another warehouse.

- Payments from customers are entered.

- Orders for delivery are processed.

- Shortages of supplies are identified by monitoring the stock.

Figure 2.3 shows with Quest Software's Benchmark Factory® the number of bytes processed by each TPC-C transaction when running different number of user loads with a TPC-C database of 10 GB. Beside the number of bytes processed, Benchmark Factory provides transaction time, response time, number of rows processed and other performance metrics for TPC-C transactions.

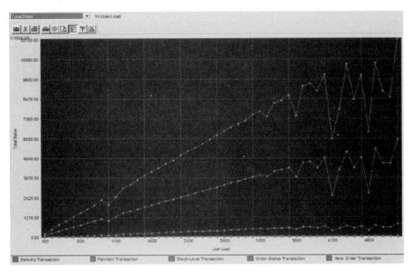

**Figure 2.3:** *Benchmark Factory reports the number of bytes processed by each TPC-C transaction in a TPC-C database of 10 GB.*

TPC-C transactions run on a database composed of nine different tables. Figure 2.4 shows the entity-relationship diagram created with the Toad™ Data Modeler tool for the TPC-C tables with data population requirements. In Figure 2.4, 'W' represents a Warehouse. The numbers within the parenthesis in the entity boxes indicate the cardinality in number of rows factored by 'W' number of warehouses. The numbers by the relationships indicate the cardinality between the parent and child tables. The plus sign (+) indicates that cardinality may vary in the initial database population as rows are added or deleted.

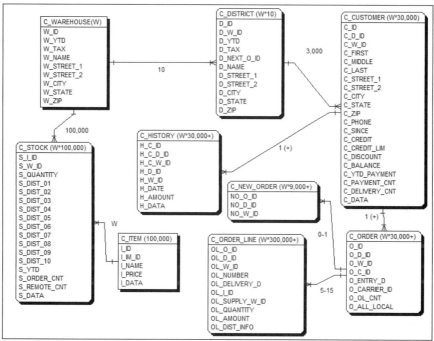

**Figure 2.4:** *TPC-C Database Entity-Relationship Diagram.*

TPC-C is measured in transactions per minute (tpmC) which indicates new order transactions executed per minute and provides a measure of business throughput.

Benchmark Factory creates a TPC-C database according to the data population requirements. In Benchmark Factory you can indicate the scale factor for the benchmark. The scale factor determines the amount of data initially loaded into the benchmark tables. For the TPC-C benchmark, each scale factor represents one warehouse. A maximum of 10 users should be run against each warehouse. For example, user loads of 1, 5, and 10 set the scale to 1. If using other user load values, the scale factor should be changed accordingly. Figure 4.5 illustrates the database explosion wizard for the TPC-C benchmark in Benchmark Factory with table sizes according to the specified scale factor.

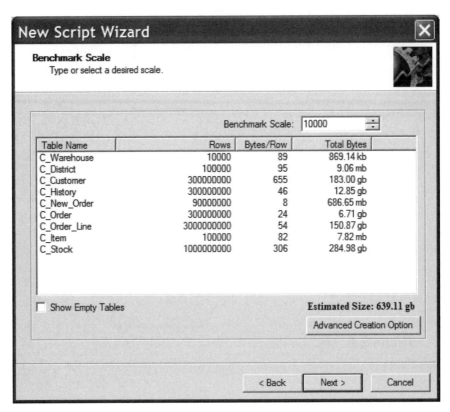

**Figure 2.5:** *Scale factor in Benchmark Factory allows you to easily indicate TPC-C benchmark database size.*

There are some best practices when performing database benchmarks to keep in mind:

- Benchmarking on a production server significantly degrades performance or even can cause the system to fail. When benchmarking it is always advisable to use a test system, or test when no applications are running on the database and have a recovery plan.

- Back-up the database prior testing in case of system failure.

- Before running a benchmark again, restore the database to the initialize state.

The following are best practices specific to the TPC-C benchmark:

- Latencies between transactions are indicated in the TPC-C specification. When using a tool like Benchmark Factory, if you change latency values, test runs can be different and low latency values could create excessive locking in the database due to the nature of the TPC-C transactions.

- Select the right benchmark database scale for the number of users to simulate, i.e. 1 scale to 10 users maximum.

# TPC-H

TPC-H, the evolution of the former TPC-D benchmark, is a decision support benchmark designed to run queries when the system does not know what transactions the users will run. This benchmark's ad-hoc query nature illustrates decision support systems with large volumes of data. TPC-H is a data warehousing benchmark, and benchmark databases are typically very large (which could cause tests to take long a time to run – refer to chapter 6 for recommendations to speed up TPC-H). The minimum database required to run the TPC-H benchmark holds business data from 10,000 suppliers and contains ten million rows representing a raw storage capacity of about 1 GB.

In Benchmark Factory the database professional can indicate the scale factor for the TPC-H database to control the size of the database. TPC-H goes from scale factors 1, 10, 30, 100, 300, 1000, 3000, 10000, 30000, 100000, 300000, 100000 for a database size from 1GB to 100TB.

TPC-H results are reported as *Composite Query-per-Hour Performance Metric* (QphH@Size). This metric reflects multiple aspects of the database such as database size, query processing power when they are executed in by only one user or multiple concurrent users. Comparisons of TPC-H results should be done using same size databases.

TPC-H is composed by 22 transactions and two database refresh functions. The TPC-H transactions model information analysis applications and does not represent the activity of any specific business sector. The TPC-H benchmark simulates the activity of a wholesale supplier system, which runs on a database available 27x7, running multiple users who generate most of the ad-hoc queries through graphical user interfaces; batch data refresh operations for the OLTP system. This process occurs typically during maintenance periods while the DSS queries are executed.

The TPC-H benchmark is made up of two tests:

- Power Test – A single user which executes all the transactions in a set order.

- Throughput Test – Multiple users which execute all the transactions in a set order.

The TPC-H database consists of eight individual tables as illustrated in the entity-relationship diagram in Figure 2.6, created with the Toad™ Data Modeler tool. The numbers within parenthesis by the table name indicate the cardinality in number of rows, and *ScaleF* indicates the data proportion between tables when the database size grows.

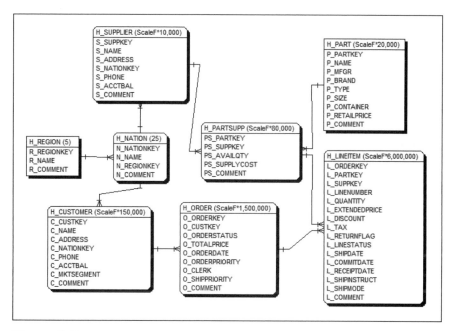

**Figure 2.6:** *TPC-H Database Entity-Relationship Diagram.*

# TPC-E

TPC-E is a new OLTP benchmark being developed by the TPC. The TPC-E benchmark is designed to simulate OLTP workload of a brokerage firm. TPC-E is the evolution of the TPC-C benchmark created 14 years ago. Although server hardware has changed dramatically since 1992, the TPC-C benchmark has not evolved at the same speed as the server industry. TPC-E is designed to be more representative of the modern database servers, less expensive to run and less susceptible to variation in scores caused by hardware and software configurations. TPC-E is still under draft and has not been officially released by TPC as of early Q3 2006.

# AS3AP & Scalable Hardware

The ANSI SQL Standard Scalable and Portable (AS3AP) benchmark is designed to provide a true apples-to-apples comparison between different relational database systems. AS3AP provides a set of tests for database processing power which is scalable and portable, so it can be used to test a broad range of database systems.

For a particular database management system, the AS3AP benchmark determines an equivalent database size for which the system is able to execute the specified set of AS3AP tests in under 12 hours. AS3AP include single-user test scenarios which define the basic functions that a RDBMS must support as defined by the ANSI SQL Standard; and multi-user tests which establish maximum throughput for OLTP systems, measures degradation in response time and measures RDBMS performance.

The AS3AP database is designed to test special queries, to test database query optimization such as correct optimization in the presence of non-uniform distributions, correlated attributes, bind variables, join-aggregates, recursive queries and other complex queries. One requirement of AS3AP is that all single and multi-users tests should run in a total time of less than 12 hours.

The *Scalable Hardware* benchmark is a subset of the AS3AP benchmark designed to test CPU, Disk, Network, and any combination of them.

In Benchmark Factory you can create an AS3AP and Scalable Hardware benchmarks and indicate the size of the benchmark databases. For the Scalable Hardware benchmark each scale factor represents one user accessing the system. For each user a separate set of data must be created, therefore the size of the database to create should be the number of maximum user load.

# Benchmarking with a Custom Workload

Even industry standard benchmarks provide a good approach to measure performance and compare different systems. When evaluating new database versions, new database patches, database configurations, and new server platforms, the most accurate benchmark for a database is the one that uses a real production workload.

To benchmark with a custom production workload:

1. Record production activity.

2. Back-up the test database.

3. Replay the production activity against test system A to create a performance baseline.

4. If testing against the same database, for example before and after changing database configurations, the database must be restored to the initial state before running a new test. Before running a new test, keep a back-up.

5. Replay the production activity against test system B.

6. Compare test results for test system A and B.

This process can be repeated for multiple tests runs.

Production activity can be recorded directly in the database server. In SQL Server the Microsoft's SQL Server Profiler can be used to create a trace table. In Oracle, production activity can be recorded by enabling tracing. Tracing records all SQL statements executed, including concurrency between sessions, session activity, latencies and bind variable information. To activate tracing in Oracle, use the following command:

```
ALTER SYSTEM SET EVENTS '10046 trace name context forever,    level
4'
```

Oracle tracing level 4 or above records bind variable values.

Benchmark Factory allows you to replay SQL Server Profiler and Oracle traces against a test database. Benchmark Factory creates users and transactions exactly as they were executed in production preserving session currencies, latencies and bind variables data.

## Conclusion

Database benchmarking offers repeatable, predictable and measurable results that can be used to perform an apples-to-apples comparison between different platforms, databases, and system configurations. In this chapter several industry standard benchmarks such as TPC-C and TPC-H were discussed. However, the most accurate benchmarking for the database is one that compares database performance under real production workload. Benchmark Factory offers out-of-the-box industry standard benchmarks tests and allows you to replay production workload in Oracle and SQL Server.

# Capacity Planning
# Analysis

## Introduction

"Engineering is not merely knowing and being knowledgeable, like
a walking encyclopedia; engineering is not merely analysis;
engineering is not merely the possession of the capacity to get
elegant solutions to non-existent engineering problems;
engineering is practicing the art of the organized forcing of
technological change... Engineers operate at the interface between
science and society..."

Dean Gordon Brown

In this chapter, the basis for predictive modeling relating to databases will be examined. Database professionals should have the ability to predict operating system memory needs, operating system CPU needs, and operating system storage requirements. The analysis may be as simple as answering the question, "When will this table run out of space?" or as complex as, "How many CPUs will be required to support this database when the data has increased by a factor of 20 in size and user load has been increased ten fold?".

In order to accurately model databases to allow the prediction of future needs based on current trends, database administrators must be able to control two specific parts of the database environment:

- User load

- Transaction mix

If database administrators cannot control the users or the transactions impacting the database, then it becomes impossible to accurately predict the trends. However, if average loads and normal data growth are the concern, then when measurements are performed the administrator must ensure that the transaction mix and user load is "normal." If a normal load measurement is not known, then these efforts will probably result in inaccurate forecasts based on biased trends.

One way to completely control both the users and the transaction load is to utilize benchmarking tools. The benchmarking tools presented in the next section can be utilized by the database professional to perform accurate trend analysis and prediction.

## Trend Identification

If all that benchmarking tools did were standard canned benchmarks, they would be of limited use for trend analysis. Top of the line tools such as Benchmark Factory from Quest provide utilities that allow the reading of trace files from databases such as Oracle and the entry of SQL statements to test transactions for other database systems. In addition, the tools should allow for the specification of multiple user scenarios so that insert, update, delete as well as select transactions can be modeled.

A test case will be used to determine if a particular set of transactions have an effect on the number of users that can select from the view as well as how many users can perform DML operations while users are performing selects against the materialized views. The test case will look specifically at Data Manipulation Language (DML) transactions to the base tables for an Oracle materialized view. A materialized view is a "instantiated" view that is used to create and maintain an actual physical table so that its records stay in sync with its base tables.

## Testing an Architecture

One of the suggested architectures to allow for rapid reporting without stressing the base tables is to use partitioned, refresh on commit, materialized views within Oracle. This test should help show the affects of user load on such an architecture.

In order to test this architecture, the Quest Benchmark Factory was utilized with two GUI installations; one to do the *INSERT* into the base tables, the other to perform the *SELECT* activity against the refresh on commit materialized view. The testing was performed in three phases:

- **Phase 1:** In phase 1 both the INSERT and SELECT potions of the test were cycled simultaneously from 1-60 users in 5 user increments on the INSERT side and 1-30 users in 5 user increments on the SELECT side.

- **Phase 2:** In phase 2 the INSERT side was cycled from 1-60 users in 5 user increments until the response time exceeded 6 seconds while the SELECT side was run at a single constant user level during individual INSERT runs. The SELECT side was run at constant user levels of 5, 10 and 20 users during the INSERT tests.

- **Phase 3:** In phase 3 the materialized view was recreated as a single table and the constant user level of 20 for SELECTs was used to test the difference between use of partitions and single tables.

In all phases, the SALES table was used for the update target with ON COMMIT processing for the materialized views causing selects from all the base tables in the PUBS schema (SALES, AUTHOR, BOOK, AUTHOR_BOOK, PUBLISHER, STORE) to publish data into the *mv_author_sales* materialized view. In Oracle, ON COMMIT processing means just that, whenever there is a commit on the base tables, the effected materialized view records are updated, inserted or deleted.

Prior to each test the *mv_author_sales* materialized view and the SALES table were both truncated.

## System Information

The test system consisted of two laptops each configured with the Benchmark Factory utility.

- Laptop 1, a VIO PCG-GRT250P with a, 2.8 Ghz Pentium IV processor, 1 gigabyte of memory, and a 1 GigaBit Ethernet card was used for running the *INSERT* processing.

- Laptop 2, a Gateway 9300 with a 400 Mhz PII processor, 700 Megabytes of memory, and a 100 Megabit Ethernet card was used for the *SELECT* processing.

The database server is a Redhat Linux based 3.0 Ghz Pentium IV with hyperthreading and 2 Gigabytes of memory running Oracle Enterprise 10gR2 10.1.0.3 release. The server is directly attached through Fast-Wide SCSI to an 8 disk NStore disk array using all 8-19 Gigabyte 10K rpm drives in a RAID5 array. This architecture is shown in Figure 3.1.

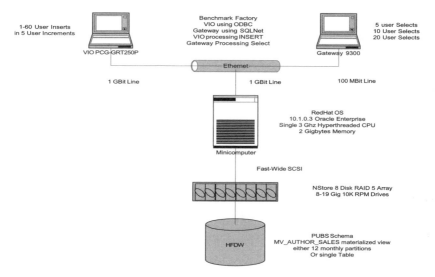

**Figure 3.1:** *Test Architecture*

# Database Objects

The database utilizes a base set of tables, SALES, AUTHOR, BOOK, AUTHOR_BOOK, STORE and PUBLISHER. These tables are used to create a REFRESH-ON-COMMIT materialized view constructed on top of an existing partitioned table.

## Details of Materialized View

The script used to create the materialized view base partitioned table is shown below:

```
drop materialized view mv_author_sales;
drop table mv_author_sales;
truncate table sales;
CREATE TABLE mv_author_sales
      PARTITION BY RANGE (order_date)
         (PARTITION p1  VALUES LESS THAN
(to_date('012002','mmyyyy')),
            PARTITION p2  VALUES LESS THAN
(to_date('022002','mmyyyy')),
            PARTITION p3  VALUES LESS THAN
(to_date('032002','mmyyyy')),
            PARTITION p4  VALUES LESS THAN
(to_date('042002','mmyyyy')),
            PARTITION p5  VALUES LESS THAN
(to_date('052002','mmyyyy')),
            PARTITION p6  VALUES LESS THAN
(to_date('062002','mmyyyy')),
            PARTITION p7  VALUES LESS THAN
(to_date('072002','mmyyyy')),
            PARTITION p8  VALUES LESS THAN
(to_date('082002','mmyyyy')),
            PARTITION p9  VALUES LESS THAN
(to_date('092002','mmyyyy')),
            PARTITION p10 VALUES LESS THAN
(to_date('102002','mmyyyy')),
            PARTITION p11 VALUES LESS THAN
(to_date('112002','mmyyyy')),
            PARTITION p12 VALUES LESS THAN
(to_date('122002','mmyyyy')),
            PARTITION p13 VALUES LESS THAN (MAXVALUE))
as
(Select d.order_date,
a.rowid idrowa, b.rowid idrowb, c.rowid idrowc,
d.rowid idrowd, e.rowid idrowe, f.rowid idrowf,
a.author_last_name, a.author_first_name,f.pub_name,
a.author_contract_nbr,
e.store_state,d.quantity
From author a, book_author b, book c, sales d, store e, publisher f
Where a.author_key=b.author_key
And b.book_key=c.book_key And c.book_key=d.book_key
And e.store_key=d.store_key
and c.pub_key=f.pub_key)
/
create index mv_rida on mv_author_sales(idrowa);
create index mv_ridb on mv_author_sales(idrowb);
create index mv_ridc on mv_author_sales(idrowc);
create index mv_ridd on mv_author_sales(idrowd);
create index mv_ride on mv_author_sales(idrowe);
create index mv_ridf on mv_author_sales(idrowf);
```

Once the base table is created, the materialized view is defined on the existing table. The script used to create the materialized view is shown as follows:

```
Create materialized view  mv_author_sales
on prebuilt table
Refresh on commit
as
Select d.order_date,a.rowid idrowa, b.rowid idrowb, c.rowid idrowc,
d.rowid idrowd, e.rowid idrowe, f.rowid idrowf, a.author_last_name,
a.author_first_name,f.pub_name,
a.author_contract_nbr,
e.store_state,d.quantity
From author a, book_author b, book c, sales d, store e, publisher f
Where a.author_key=b.author_key
And b.book_key=c.book_key And c.book_key=d.book_key
And e.store_key=d.store_key
and c.pub_key=f.pub_key
/
```

After creation and refreshing, the MV_AUTHOR_SALES and SALES tables were analyzed using a command similar to:

```
dbms_stats.gather_table_stats('PUBS','MV_AUTHOR_SALES',cascade=>true
);
```

The dynamic sampling feature of 10g was utilized to maintain statistics for the test since the table and materialized view were growing during the entire test period for each test.

## Transaction Details

Two basic transactions were utilized to test the affect of locking on the INSERT and SELECT activities. The SALES table formed the base of the materialized view *mv_author_sales* so the INSERT transaction focused on inserts into the SALES table. The inserts into the SALES table force the materialized view refresh (*REFRESH-ON-COMMT*) to select records from all of the base tables. The following Benchmark Factory function scripts where used to populate random values into the *INSERT* statement:

- **$BFRandList** – Insert one of the provided lists into the statement at this point with frequency based on the provided integer ("val":f). If no integer is provided, use 1.

- **$BFRandRange** – Insert a random integer in the range specified.

- **$BFDate** – Insert a random date in the range specified.

## Insert Transaction

```
INSERT INTO sales VALUES (
'$BFRandList("S101","S103","S103","S104","S105","S106","S107","S108"
,
"S109","S110")',
'$BFRandList("B101","B102","B103","B104","B105","B106","B107","B108"
,"B109","B110","B111","B112","B113","B114","B115","B116")',
 'O'||to_char(order_number.nextval),
 to_date('$BFDate("01/01/2002","12/31/2002")','mm/dd/yyyy'),
 $BFRandRange(1,100));
```

The *SELECT* transaction was designed to fully access the materialized view, placing the most stress on the view as possible.

## Select Transaction

```
SELECT to_number(to_char(order_date,'mmyyyy'))
month_of_sales,author_first_name,author_last_name,sum(quantity) FROM
mv_author_sales
GROUP BY
to_number(to_char(order_date,'mmyyyy')),author_first_name,author_las
t_name;
```

Using *INSERT* with the Benchmark Factory script functions provided a distribution of values similar to the following example distribution in all the tests.

| PARTITION | COUNT(*) |
|-----------|----------|
| 012002 | 831 |
| 022002 | 765 |
| 032002 | 805 |
| 042002 | 799 |
| 052002 | 885 |
| 062002 | 788 |
| 072002 | 896 |
| 082002 | 864 |
| 092002 | 871 |
| 102002 | 843 |
| 112002 | 888 |
| 122002 | 857 |

The next sections show the results from the three phases of testing.

# Phase 1:

## Insert & Select Varying

In phase 1, both Benchmark Factory tests were made to scale. From 1-30 users for selects in 5 user increments (1, 5, 10, 15, 20, 25, 30) and 1-60 users in inserts in 5 user increments. During testing locks were monitored using the following procedure.

```
Create or replace procedure get_locks(tim_in_min number) as
interations number;
I integer;
begin
interations:=floor(tim_in_min*60/4)+1;
for I in 1..interations
loop
insert into perm4_object_locks
select sysdate, b.object_name,count(*)
 from v$locked_object a, dba_objects b
 where a.object_id=b.object_id
 and object_name!='PERM4_OBJECT_LOCKS'
 group by object_name;
commit;
dbms_lock.sleep(4);
end loop;
end;
```

The locking was monitored at 4 second intervals and the results for Phase 1, 1-30 User *SELECT* processes in 5 user increments versus *INSERT* processing at 1-60 users in 5 user increments.

The following is the lock profile for the *mv_author_sales* materialized view:

```
MEAS_ OBJECT_NAME      SUM(NUM_LOCKS)
----- ---------------  --------------
21:10 MV_AUTHOR_SALES               2
21:11 MV_AUTHOR_SALES               4
21:12 MV_AUTHOR_SALES               2
21:13 MV_AUTHOR_SALES               2
```

```
21:14 MV_AUTHOR_SALES          4
21:17 MV_AUTHOR_SALES          2
21:18 MV_AUTHOR_SALES          2
21:19 MV_AUTHOR_SALES          2
21:21 MV_AUTHOR_SALES          3
21:22 MV_AUTHOR_SALES          4
21:23 MV_AUTHOR_SALES          2
21:25 MV_AUTHOR_SALES          2
```

The INSERT side of the test results is shown in Figure 3.2.

| General Information | | | |
|---|---|---|---|
| **Run Information** | | | |
| Test Run Id | 71 | Status | Completed |
| Start Time | 3/10/2006 21:10 | Stop Time | 3/10/2006 21:26 |
| Comment | Insert 1-60 by 5 | | |

| Profile Information | |
|---|---|
| Profile Name | aultdb2 |
| Driver | ODBC |
| Data Source Name | TEST |
| User Name | Pubs |
| Password | ****** |

| Test Information | | | |
|---|---|---|---|
| Name: | Response < 6000 ms (1-60 by 5) | | |
| Test Type: | Mixed Workload Database Test | | |
| Test Id: | 5 | Version | 11 |

| Overall Results | | | | | | |
|---|---|---|---|---|---|---|
| Userload | Test Phase | TPS | Avg Time | Min Time | Max Time | 90th Time |
| 1 | 1 | 6.02 | 0.165 | 0.098 | 0.316 | 0.213 |
| 5 | 1 | 4.41 | 1.133 | 0.534 | 3.361 | 1.535 |

| 10 | 1 | 3.02 | 3.306 | 1.993 | 5.377 | 3.922 |
|----|---|------|-------|-------|--------|--------|
| 15 | 1 | 2.24 | 6.684 | 3.534 | 22.143 | 11.004 |

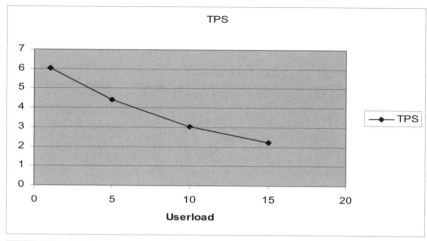

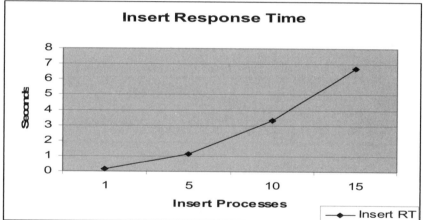

**Figure 3.2:** *Results for INSERT Test*

The results for the SELECT test of Phase 1 are shown in Figure 3.3.

General Information

Run Information

## General Information

| | | | |
|---|---|---|---|
| Test Run Id | 11 | Status | Completed |
| Start Time | 3/10/2006 21:01 | Stop Time | 3/10/2006 21:29 |
| Comment | SELECT 1-30 by 5 | | |

## Profile Information

| | |
|---|---|
| Profile Name | aultdb2 |
| Driver | Oracle |
| Net Service Name | TEST |
| Tablespace | Users |
| User Name | Pubs |
| Password | ****** |

## Test Information

| | |
|---|---|
| Name: | Max TPS (1-30 by 5) |
| Test Type: | Mixed Workload Database Test |
| Test Id: | 2        Version    4 |

## Overall Results

| User load | Test Phase | TPS | Avg Time | Min Time | Max Time | 90th Time |
|---|---|---|---|---|---|---|
| 1 | 1 | 3.34 | 0.298 | 0.23 | 0.64 | 0.334 |
| 5 | 1 | 8.69 | 0.575 | 0.346 | 0.935 | 0.676 |
| 10 | 1 | 12.04 | 0.829 | 0.393 | 1.627 | 1.005 |
| 15 | 1 | 13.42 | 1.116 | 0.401 | 2.916 | 1.457 |
| 20 | 1 | 15.67 | 1.274 | 0.594 | 2.758 | 1.565 |
| 25 | 1 | 16.04 | 1.556 | 0.84 | 3.672 | 2.014 |
| 30 | 1 | 16.09 | 1.862 | 0.923 | 6.392 | 2.469 |

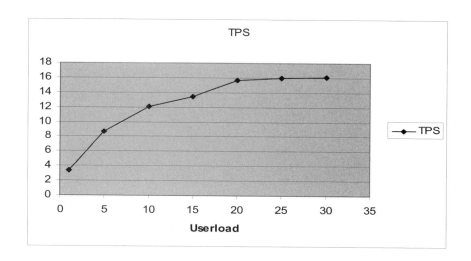

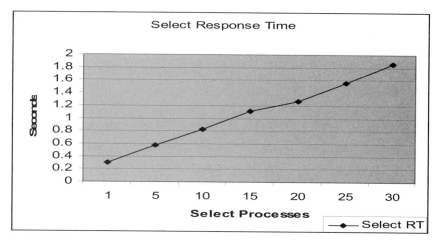

**Figure 3.3:** *Select Test Results*

Over all, the results for Phase 1 show that the locking affects INSERT processing resulting in the average time for inserts to increase to greater than 6 seconds within 15 user processes; while SELECT processing shows little affect other than that which can be expected from the materialized view table size increase. However, the effects are difficult to characterize when both INSERT and SELECT processes are varying.

## Phase 2:
## SELECT Transaction Level Constant

In Phase 2 the transaction levels for SELECTs were held at constant levels (5, 10, 20), and TPS and response were checked for Inserts (levels 1-60 or where Response >6 sec.)

In Phase 2 testing the number of SELECT user processes was kept at constant values while the number of INSERT processes was increased in 5 user intervals until response time increase above 6 seconds. SELECT user levels of 5, 10 and 20 were used. The TPS and response time for the SELECT processes were recorded at each user level for each upward increment in the number of INSERT processes to gauge the affect of increased locking on the SELECT processing.

## 5 Concurrent SELECTS

With 1, 5, 10, 15, 20, 25, 30 INSERT operations at 4-5 minute interval ramp recorded >3 sec response at 20 users, >6 sec response at 30 users test was halted when insert processing reached >6 seconds transaction time. The results for the INSERT processing are shown in Figure 3.4.

| General Information | | | |
|---|---|---|---|
| Run Information | | | |
| Test Run Id | 78 | Status | Completed |
| Start Time | 3/11/2006 20:50 | Stop Time | 3/11/2006 21:19 |
| Comment | 5 Selects | | |

| Profile Information | |
|---|---|
| Profile Name | aultdb2 |

| General Information | | | | | |
|---|---|---|---|---|---|
| Driver | ODBC | | | | |
| Data Source Name | TEST | | | | |
| User Name | Pubs | | | | |
| Password | ****** | | | | |

| Userload | Test Phase | TPS | Avg Time | Min Time | Max Time | 90th Time |
|---|---|---|---|---|---|---|
| 1 | 1 | 5.79 | 0.172 | 0.113 | 0.287 | 0.225 |
| 5 | 1 | 6.29 | 0.795 | 0.517 | 2.675 | 0.978 |
| 10 | 1 | 4.32 | 2.315 | 1.262 | 7.888 | 3.732 |
| 15 | 1 | 5.56 | 2.699 | 1.798 | 3.97 | 3.243 |
| 20 | 1 | 5.43 | 3.681 | 2.572 | 5.699 | 4.37 |
| 25 | 1 | 5.01 | 4.993 | 3.439 | 10.602 | 5.672 |
| 30 | 1 | 4.82 | 6.23 | 4.471 | 30.898 | 9.358 |

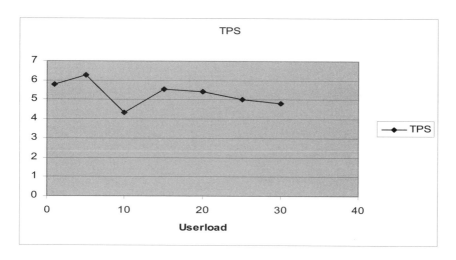

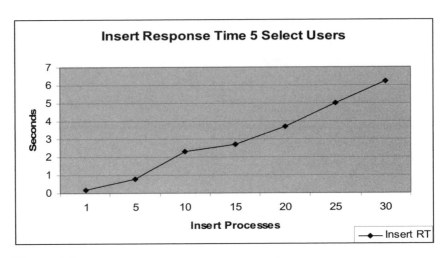

**Figure 3.4:** *Results from 5 Select processes on Inserts*

The resulting lock profile from the inserts is shown as follows:

```
MEAS_ OBJECT_NAME       SUM(NUM_LOCKS)
----- ---------------   --------------
20:50 MV_AUTHOR_SALES                6
20:51 MV_AUTHOR_SALES                6
20:52 MV_AUTHOR_SALES                4
20:53 MV_AUTHOR_SALES                2
20:54 MV_AUTHOR_SALES                6
20:55 MV_AUTHOR_SALES                6
20:56 MV_AUTHOR_SALES                6
20:58 MV_AUTHOR_SALES                2
20:59 MV_AUTHOR_SALES                2
21:00 MV_AUTHOR_SALES                1
21:01 MV_AUTHOR_SALES                4
21:02 MV_AUTHOR_SALES                4
21:03 MV_AUTHOR_SALES                4
21:04 MV_AUTHOR_SALES                4
21:05 MV_AUTHOR_SALES                2
21:06 MV_AUTHOR_SALES                2
21:07 MV_AUTHOR_SALES                4
21:08 MV_AUTHOR_SALES                2
21:09 MV_AUTHOR_SALES                4
21:10 MV_AUTHOR_SALES                2
21:11 MV_AUTHOR_SALES                6
21:12 MV_AUTHOR_SALES                2
21:13 MV_AUTHOR_SALES                2
21:14 MV_AUTHOR_SALES                4
21:15 MV_AUTHOR_SALES                5
21:16 MV_AUTHOR_SALES                2
21:17 MV_AUTHOR_SALES                2
21:18 MV_AUTHOR_SALES                6
```

# 10 Concurrent SELECTS

With 1, 5, 10, 15, 20, 25, 30 INSERT operations at 4-5 minute interval ramp recorded >3 sec response at 20 users, >6 sec response at 30 users test was halted when insert processing reached >6 seconds transaction time. The results for the INSERT processing are shown in Figure 3.5.

| General Information | | | |
|---|---|---|---|
| Run Information | | | |
| Test Run Id | 73 | Status | Completed |
| Start Time | 3/11/2006 18:59 | Stop Time | 3/11/2006 19:28 |
| Comment | 10 Selects | | |

| Profile Information | |
|---|---|
| Profile Name | aultdb2 |
| Driver | ODBC |
| Data Source Name | TEST |
| User Name | Pubs |
| Password | ****** |

| Userload | Test Phase | TPS | Avg Time | Min Time | Max Time | 90th Time |
|---|---|---|---|---|---|---|
| 1 | 1 | 5.44 | 0.183 | 0.118 | 0.293 | 0.238 |
| 5 | 1 | 6.02 | 0.83 | 0.543 | 2.688 | 1.006 |
| 10 | 1 | 5.51 | 1.814 | 1.203 | 3.043 | 2.287 |
| 15 | 1 | 5.12 | 2.93 | 1.946 | 5.013 | 3.547 |
| 20 | 1 | 4.9 | 4.077 | 2.774 | 9.723 | 4.858 |
| 25 | 1 | 4.4 | 5.678 | 3.837 | 20.626 | 7.881 |
| 30 | 1 | 4.07 | 7.369 | 4.753 | 40.996 | 12.639 |

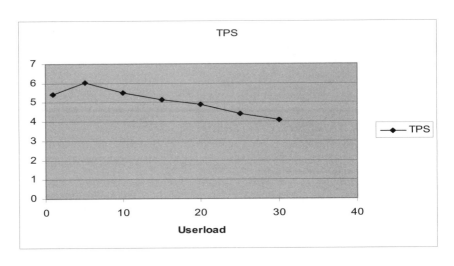

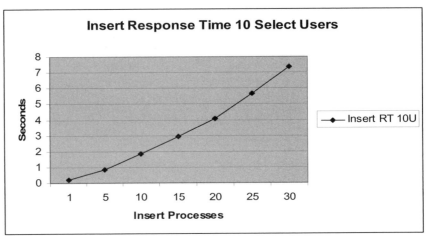

**Figure 3.5:** *Results from 10 SELECT Users on INSERTs*

The resulting lock profile from the inserts is shown as follows:

```
MEAS_  OBJECT_NAME      SUM(NUM_LOCKS)
-----  ---------------  --------------
18:59  MV_AUTHOR_SALES               4
19:00  MV_AUTHOR_SALES               2
19:02  MV_AUTHOR_SALES               8
19:04  MV_AUTHOR_SALES               5
19:05  MV_AUTHOR_SALES               2
19:06  MV_AUTHOR_SALES               4
```

```
19:07 MV_AUTHOR_SALES          4
19:08 MV_AUTHOR_SALES          4
19:09 MV_AUTHOR_SALES          4
19:10 MV_AUTHOR_SALES          6
19:12 MV_AUTHOR_SALES          4
19:13 MV_AUTHOR_SALES          4
19:15 MV_AUTHOR_SALES          6
19:16 MV_AUTHOR_SALES          4
19:18 MV_AUTHOR_SALES          2
19:19 MV_AUTHOR_SALES          4
19:20 MV_AUTHOR_SALES          2
19:21 MV_AUTHOR_SALES          2
19:22 MV_AUTHOR_SALES          6
19:24 MV_AUTHOR_SALES          2
19:25 MV_AUTHOR_SALES          2
19:26 MV_AUTHOR_SALES          4
19:27 MV_AUTHOR_SALES          2
```

## 12 Concurrent SELECTS

With 1, 5, 10, 15, 20, 25 *INSERT* operations at 4-5 minute interval ramp recorded >3 sec response at 15 users, >6 sec response at 25 users test was halted when insert processing reached >6 seconds transaction time. The results for the *INSERT* processing are shown in Figure 3.6.

| General Information | | | |
|---|---|---|---|
| Run Information | | | |
| Test Run Id | 76 | Status | Completed |
| Start Time | 3/11/2006 19:51 | Stop Time | 3/11/2006 20:16 |
| Comment | 20 Selects | | |
| | | | |
| Profile Information | | | |
| Profile Name | aultdb2 | | |
| Driver | ODBC | | |
| Data Source Name | TEST | | |
| User Name | Pubs | | |

| Password | ****** |
| --- | --- |

| Userload | Test Phase | TPS | Avg Time | Min Time | Max Time | 90th Time |
| --- | --- | --- | --- | --- | --- | --- |
| 1 | 1 | 5.12 | 0.195 | 0.123 | 0.52 | 0.249 |
| 5 | 1 | 6.02 | 0.829 | 0.491 | 3.122 | 1.032 |
| 10 | 1 | 5.4 | 1.852 | 1.214 | 2.992 | 2.296 |
| 15 | 1 | 4.93 | 3.042 | 2.027 | 5.43 | 3.613 |
| 20 | 1 | 4.53 | 4.418 | 2.929 | 9.93 | 5.168 |
| 25 | 1 | 3.86 | 6.47 | 4.015 | 31.277 | 10.115 |

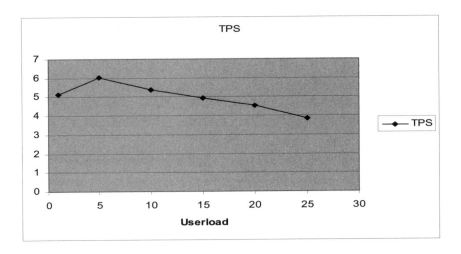

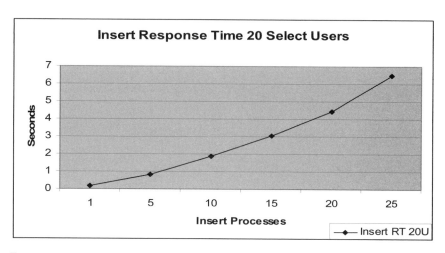

**Figure 3.6:** *Results from 20 SELECT Users on INSERTs*

The resulting lock profile from the inserts is shown as follows:.

```
MEAS_ OBJECT_NAME      SUM(NUM_LOCKS)
----- ---------------  --------------
19:52 MV_AUTHOR_SALES               2
19:53 MV_AUTHOR_SALES               4
19:55 MV_AUTHOR_SALES               2
19:56 MV_AUTHOR_SALES               6
19:57 MV_AUTHOR_SALES               6
19:58 MV_AUTHOR_SALES               4
20:00 MV_AUTHOR_SALES               4
20:01 MV_AUTHOR_SALES               4
20:02 MV_AUTHOR_SALES               4
20:04 MV_AUTHOR_SALES               4
20:05 MV_AUTHOR_SALES               4
20:07 MV_AUTHOR_SALES               4
20:08 MV_AUTHOR_SALES               4
20:09 MV_AUTHOR_SALES               2
20:11 MV_AUTHOR_SALES               8
20:13 MV_AUTHOR_SALES               2
20:14 MV_AUTHOR_SALES               2

17 rows selected.
```

Over all, the Phase 2 testing shows that locking has little or no affect on SELECT operations, while the number of SELECT processes has an affect on the number of INSERT processes capable of operating with a less than 6 second response time and the number of TPS that can be processed for that user level.

# Phase 3: Materialized View with No Partitions

In Phase 3 the effect of utilizing a single base table verses using multiple partitions at the maximum number of SELECT processes (20) is measured. The scripts used to create the single table materialized view are shown as follows:

```
CREATE TABLE mv_author_sales
as
(Select
 d.order_date,
 a.rowid idrowa,
 b.rowid idrowb,
 c.rowid idrowc,
 d.rowid idrowd,
 e.rowid idrowe,
 f.rowid idrowf,
 a.author_last_name,
 a.author_first_name,
 f.pub_name,
 a.author_contract_nbr,
 e.store_state,d.quantity
From
 author a,
 book_author b,
 book c,
 sales d,
 store e,
 publisher f
Where
 a.author_key=b.author_key
 and b.book_key=c.book_key
 and c.book_key=d.book_key
 and e.store_key=d.store_key
 and c.pub_key=f.pub_key)

create index mv_rida on mv_author_sales(idrowa);
create index mv_ridb on mv_author_sales(idrowb);
create index mv_ridc on mv_author_sales(idrowc);
create index mv_ridd on mv_author_sales(idrowd);
create index mv_ride on mv_author_sales(idrowe);
create index mv_ridf on mv_author_sales(idrowf);

Create materialized view  mv_author_sales
on prebuilt table
Refresh on commit
as
```

```
Select d.order_date,a.rowid idrowa,
b.rowid idrowb, c.rowid idrowc, d.rowid idrowd,
e.rowid idrowe, f.rowid idrowf, a.author_last_name,
a.author_first_name,f.pub_name,
a.author_contract_nbr,
e.store_state,d.quantity
From author a, book_author b, book c, sales d, store e,
publisher f
Where a.author_key=b.author_key
And b.book_key=c.book_key And c.book_key=d.book_key
And e.store_key=d.store_key
and c.pub_key=f.pub_key
/

Truncate sales and mv_author_sales

exec
dbms_stats.gather_table_stats('PUBS','MV_AUTHOR_SALES',cascade=>true
);
```

The Phase 3 results for the *INSERT* processes are shown in Figure 3.7.

| General Information | | | |
|---|---|---|---|
| **Run Information** | | | |
| Test Run Id | 79 | Status | Completed |
| Start Time | 3/12/2006 11:13 | Stop Time | 3/12/2006 0:02 |
| Comment | Non-Part table 20 concurrent SELECTS | | |

| Profile Information | |
|---|---|
| Profile Name | aultdb2 |
| Driver | ODBC |
| Data Source Name | TEST |
| User Name | Pubs |
| Password | ****** |

| Test Information | | | |
|---|---|---|---|
| Name: | Response < 6000 ms (1-60 by 5) | | |
| Test Type: | Mixed Workload Database Test | | |
| Test Id: | 5 | Version | 12 |

| Userload | Test Phase | TPS | Avg Time | Min Time | Max Time | 90th Time |
|---|---|---|---|---|---|---|
| 1 | 1 | 5 | 0.199 | 0.114 | 0.857 | 0.254 |
| 5 | 1 | 5.96 | 0.838 | 0.499 | 2.671 | 1.033 |
| 10 | 1 | 5.21 | 1.919 | 1.203 | 4.221 | 2.394 |
| 15 | 1 | 4.97 | 3.017 | 2.08 | 4.947 | 3.663 |
| 20 | 1 | 4.66 | 4.287 | 2.963 | 9.9 | 5.136 |
| 25 | 1 | 4.18 | 5.975 | 3.881 | 25.745 | 8.7 |
| 30 | 1 | 3.66 | 8.206 | 4.744 | 66.935 | 15.143 |

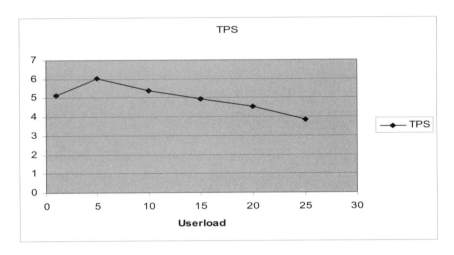

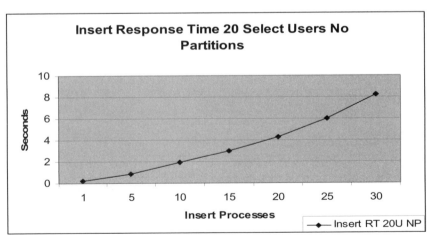

The resulting lock profile from the inserts is shown as follows:

```
TIME   OBJECT_NAME       NUM_LOCKS
-----  ----------------  ----------
11:33  MV_AUTHOR_SALES           1
11:35  MV_AUTHOR_SALES           3
11:36  MV_AUTHOR_SALES           2
11:37  MV_AUTHOR_SALES           3
11:38  MV_AUTHOR_SALES           2
11:40  MV_AUTHOR_SALES           1
11:41  MV_AUTHOR_SALES           2
11:42  MV_AUTHOR_SALES           2
11:43  MV_AUTHOR_SALES           3
11:44  MV_AUTHOR_SALES           2
11:45  MV_AUTHOR_SALES           1
11:46  MV_AUTHOR_SALES           1
11:48  MV_AUTHOR_SALES           1
11:49  MV_AUTHOR_SALES           2
11:50  MV_AUTHOR_SALES           2
11:51  MV_AUTHOR_SALES           3
11:53  MV_AUTHOR_SALES           2
11:55  MV_AUTHOR_SALES           1
11:56  MV_AUTHOR_SALES           1
11:57  MV_AUTHOR_SALES           2
11:58  MV_AUTHOR_SALES           1
11:59  MV_AUTHOR_SALES           3
12:00  MV_AUTHOR_SALES           1
12:01  MV_AUTHOR_SALES           3
12:02  MV_AUTHOR_SALES           1
```

The total row count for the single table test was 9299 vice 10092 in the partitioned testing (on the average.) The distribution of the values in the single table is shown as follows:

```
ORDER     COUNT(*)
------  ----------
012002         786
022002         692
032002         733
042002         737
052002         810
062002         722
072002         828
082002         803
092002         803
102002         781
112002         824
```

```
122002      780
```
```
12 rows selected.
```

Phase 3 shows that while partitions are good for SELECT processing, they may have a slightly detrimental affect on INSERT processing. The INSERT processing affects may be mitigated by changing how rows are stored in the table such as by large PCTFREE allocations limiting the rows per block.

## Combined Results

It is easier to see the effects of the increasing number of SELECT processes by combining the results from the various tests into a series of graphs. The first graph shows the affect on transactions per second (TPS). Figure 3.8 shows the combined TPS graphs for the 5, 10, 20 SELECT users and the 20 SELECT users with no partitions test results.

Notice how the performance for the 20 SELECT user no partitions TPS is less than for the 20 SELECT user partitioned results. All of the other results show the affect of the increase stress of the SELECT processing on the INSERT users and the lack of affect of the INSERT processes on the SELECT users.

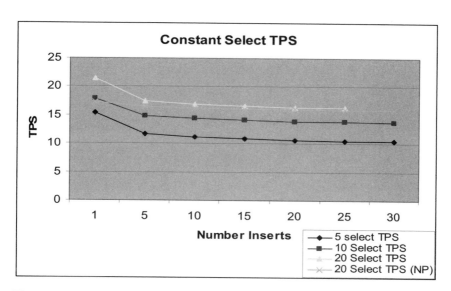

**Figure 3.8:** *Combined TPS Results*

In the next figure, Figure 3.9, the results from the response times for the SELECT processes as the number of INSERT processes increased is shown for each of the constant process levels (5, 10, 20, and 20 with no partitioning). This figure reveals that after an initial drop off, the response times showed only marginal reductions, which can probably be accredited to the increasing size of the materialized view.

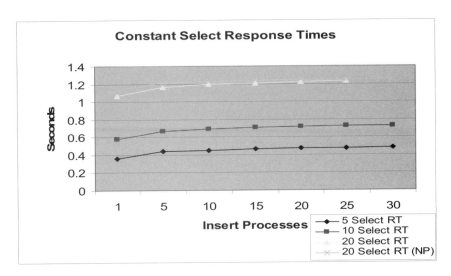

**Figure 3.9:** *Combined Response Time Results*

Figure 3.10 shows the combined results for the INSERT processing TPS as the SELECT user loads remained constant at the 5, 10 and 20 SELECT user level and 20 SELECT users with no partitioning. It further shows that for insert processing the TPS for the 20 user non-partitioned table was slightly better than for that of the 20 user partitioned table.

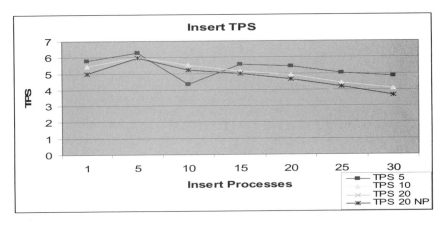

**Figure 3.10:** *Combined Insert TPS Results*

Figure 3.11 shows the affects of the varying SELECT user loads on INSERT process response times, and reveals that for the INSERT processing the response times for the 20 user non-partitioned SELECT user load are slightly better.

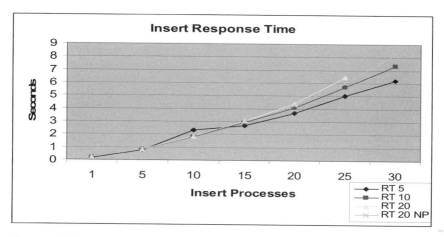

**Figure 3.11:** *Combined Insert Response Results*

# Combined Results Summary

Again, these results show that locking, as expected, has little affect on SELECT processing since with Oracle's single row (fine grained) locking model and multi-block concurrency model, readers will not be blocked by writers and writers will not be blocked by readers. It also shows that using the REFRESH ON COMMIT materialized views should not adversely affect INSERT or SELECT processing. Furthermore, the tests seem to indicate that for SELECT processing using partitions is beneficial but for INSERT processing, at least at the single row per transaction level, the partitions may have a slightly negative affect on TPS and response time.

# Recommendations

Based on the data in this report it is recommended that partitioned materialized views using the REFRESH-ON-COMMIT refresh mechanism should be used to reduce the strain on the underlying OLTP based tables when the same database instance is used in OLTP and reporting. While using partitioned materialized views shows a slight increase in response times on INSERTS, the benefits of their use outweigh the potential down sides.

In this section, an example of utilizing a benchmarking tool to see if a particular architecture was correct for our application has been shown. The example also checked to see how the application would scale on a particular hardware setup. But how can an administrator determine if a particular hardware setup is correct? The next section answers this question with an example of the use of a benchmark tool to determine projected hardware needs based on user load and projected data size.

## Planning Future Hardware & Software Needs

Projecting future hardware and software needs require database professionals to establish what the current hardware is capable of and then based on that criteria project what hardware will be needed. An actual user test case will be used as an example. In this test case, the task is determining for a production server with 20 times more data, the number of CPUs and Memory that will be required to give performance comparable to that which is currently being experienced. Here is a look at the architecture that will be tested.

## Architecture

This test uses a SUN 480R 2-900 MHz CPU based system utilizing the Solaris 2.9 64 bit architecture with 4 gigabytes of memory. The Oracle database is at release 9.2, version 9.2.0.1 and is being served by an EMC disk array. The architecture is shown in Figure 3.12.

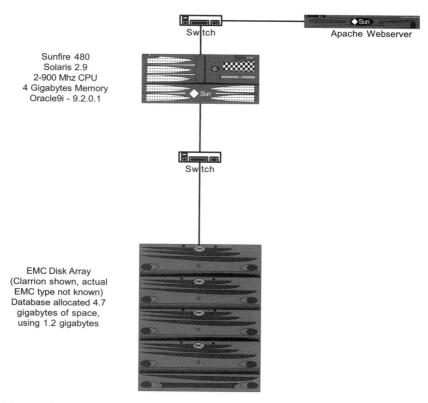

**Figure 3.12:** *Test Architecture*

# Executive Summary

Performance testing against the test table in the test database instance was accomplished during the period April 3 – April 7, 2006. The Benchmark Factory tool from Quest Software was utilized to simulate loads against the test database for various user loads and queries similar to those that will be generated by the reporting system against the database during normal operations.

Two general types of queries were tested during this time period, an issues type query set and a parts type query set. A basic template for each of the queries was provided by site personnel. The Benchmark Factory provided scripts were utilized to insert random values into the queries to generate the query loads. The random values used in the tool were selected from the test database instance to provide for a varying load for each type of query presented.

The testing was accomplished in three phases:

- **Phase 1:** In Phase 1 only issues queries were utilized to perform an SQL scalability test. In this phase, the user load was ramped in 6 user increments from 6 users to a maximum of 84 users. Each user was able to run any of the 6 queries at any time and no "think," "keyboard," or other delays were programmed into the scenario. Operating system statistics and STATSPACK were also used in this phase to collect additional statistics.

- **NOTE:** For the purposes of brevity in this example, phases 2 and 3 will be omitted.

## Limitations and Caveats

The testing described in this session was performed on a shared system where the team had no control over what other teams were doing on the server. Consequently, there are variations in transactions per second, transactions and bytes per second that would not be present in an isolated testing environment.

The server memory configuration was not able to be adequately tuned due to the limitations of a shared environment, so there are some physical I/Os which occur that would not have happened or would have been greatly reduced in a properly tuned environment.

Oracle9i Release 2 was used for the test environment. There are several bugs in Release 2 which caused ORA-00600 and other errors when large numbers of bind variables were utilized. The bind variables were considered "unsafe," such as to replace a string value in a LIKE statement, and *cursor_sharing* is set to SIMILAR.

## Phase 1: Issues Query Testing

Phase 1 is a stand-alone test of the Issues queries. The user load was ramped from 6 to 84 users. It should be noted that at 78 users, the system would begin giving resource related errors and refuse further connections.

## Randomization of the Issues Queries

In Phase 1 the queries utilized by the Benchmark Factory to test the Issues table were randomized using the user identifiers from the list of users and issues shown in Table 3.1.

| USER | Issue Count |
|---------|------|
| GEORGEB | 230 |
| FRANKL | 225 |
| MIKER | 2673 |
| SAMMYJ | 417 |
| BILLYB | 460 |
| OZZYO | 354 |

**Table 3.1:** *Users and Issue Counts*

The PRODUCT was also used to help randomize the query results. The PRODUCTs shown in Table 3.2 were utilized by Benchmark Factory to randomize the queries.

| PRODUCT | Issue Count |
|---------|-------------|
| RADIOX | 3172 |
| RADIOY | 1479 |
| DVDPX | 1210 |
| CDPY | 7880 |
| CAMCDR1 | 3187 |
| CAMCDR2 | 2270 |
| VCRX | 1510 |

**Table 3.2:** *Products and Issue Counts*

The FINISHED column had the values of either NULL or LATE so both of these conditions were utilized in various queries.

At any time during the test, a user process would be executing a query using any of the above values providing a random number of return values for each unique query.

## Transaction Times for Issues Tests

The transaction times by user load provided by the various forms of the Issues query are shown in Figure 3.13.

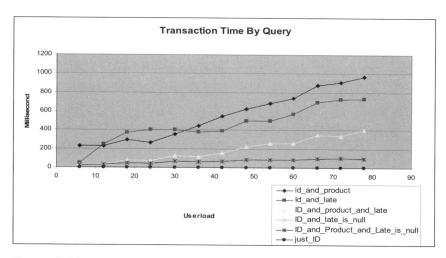

**Figure 3.13:** *Graph of Transaction Times by Query by User Load*

The data used to plot the graph in Figure 3.13 was averaged over several 78 user runs in Phase 1 and is shown in tabular form in Table 3.3.

| User Load | Id and product | Id and late | ID and product and late | ID and late is null | ID and Product and Late is null | Just ID |
|:---:|:---:|:---:|:---:|:---:|:---:|:---:|
| 6 | 228.75 | 48.75 | 29.25 | 18.25 | 22.25 | 1 |
| 12 | 227.25 | 243.5 | 38.75 | 25.25 | 27.25 | 0.75 |
| 18 | 295.5 | 373.5 | 77.25 | 39.5 | 45.5 | 1 |
| 24 | 264.25 | 401 | 73.75 | 38.75 | 44.25 | 1 |
| 30 | 353.75 | 402.5 | 126.5 | 55 | 63.5 | 1.25 |
| 36 | 442 | 377.5 | 116.25 | 54.75 | 62.5 | 1 |
| 42 | 543.5 | 390.5 | 154.75 | 60.5 | 66.75 | 1 |
| 48 | 622.25 | 498 | 220 | 75.75 | 81.75 | 1 |
| 54 | 686.5 | 498.75 | 259.25 | 79.5 | 82.5 | 1 |
| 60 | 739 | 569.5 | 255.25 | 77.5 | 81.25 | 1 |

| User Load | Id and product | Id and late | ID and product and late | ID and late is null | ID and Product and Late is null | Just ID |
|---|---|---|---|---|---|---|
| 66 | 874 | 695.75 | 347.75 | 89 | 93.75 | 1 |
| 72 | 906.5 | 723.5 | 338.25 | 96.5 | 99.5 | 1 |
| 78 | 964.25 | 733.5 | 404.5 | 96.25 | 97 | 1 |

**Table 3.3:** *Average Transaction Time in Milliseconds by Query*

The various forms of the query provided for widely varying transaction times. However, on the average, all of them are less than the specified maximum performance limit of 3 seconds.

## Average Transaction Times

The combined average transaction times are shown in Figure 3.14.

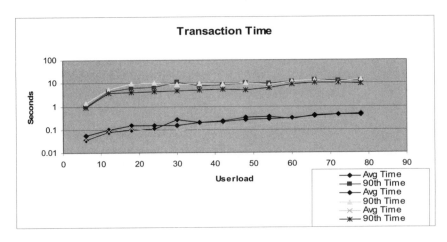

**Figure 3.14:** *Graph of Average and 90th Percentile Transaction Times*

Figure 3.14 shows that the average transaction time over all transactions per test level in each of the three phase 1 tests did not exceed 3 seconds.

Another important metric is the average response time. In a query the transaction time is the time required to generate the full transaction set, while the response time is the time required to return the first part of the result set to the user. Figure 3.15 shows the average response times for all three phase 1 tests.

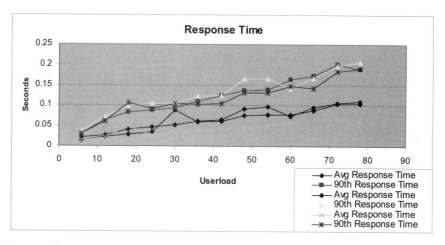

**Figure 3.15:** *Average and 90th Percentile Response Times*

The final query metric is transactions per second, otherwise called throughput. Usually one can tell when a server has reached capacity by the down turn in the TPS verses user load graph. However, due to the memory issues on the test server, enough users were not attached to reach this turnover point.

Another interesting issue with the TPS graph is the indication that the system, either at the O/S or Oracle level is undergoing throttling actions. Notice the odd down turn at around 18-24 users in the TPS graphs for two of the tests in Figure 3.16.

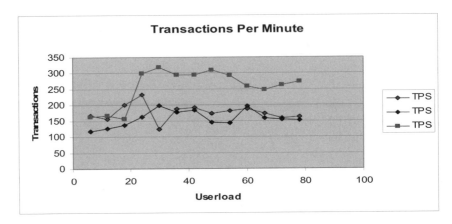

**Figure 3.16:** *Transactions per Minute*

One test has significantly higher TPS than the other two after the throttling effect at 18-24 users. This is due to the variances in server availability because of the shared user environment and makes it difficult to accurately predict overall performance for scaling purposes.

## Database Activity

Database activity levels can be shown by looking at logical reads, physical reads, and then examining the breakdown of physical reads between table scans (scattered reads) and index driven ROWID lookup reads (sequential).

In Oracle10g this data is readily available from the *dba_hist_sysstat* table by utilizing a query similar to the one shown below:

```
col meas_date format a19
set pages 0 numwidth 12
spool logical_reads_q2
select a.instance_number,to_char(a.begin_interval_time,'yyyymmdd
hh24:mi') meas_date, b.value
from dba_hist_snapshot a, dba_hist_sysstat b
where b.stat_name='session logical reads'
and a.begin_interval_time>sysdate-7
```

```
and b.snap_id=a.snap_id
order by a.instance_number,a.begin_interval_time
/
spool off
set numwidth 10 pages 22
```

Figure 3.17 shows the logical reads resulting from two of the 78 user ramp-up tests of the Issues materialized view queries. Logical reads are reads from memory requiring no physical I/O.

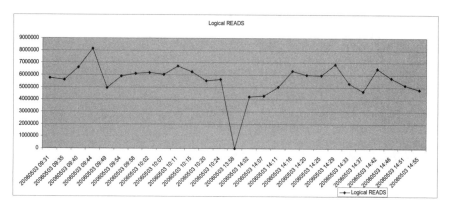

**Figure 3.17:** *Database Logical Reads*

Figure 3.17 shows that the logical reads are in the 5,000,000 to 8,000,000 range. This is data taken over intervals that span a range of user increase; the gross readings were taken at user intervals during the test. The dip to zero shows the break between the tests and is not an actual reading.

In order to put this in proper perspective, physical reads should be looked at for the same time period. This is shown in Figure 3.18.

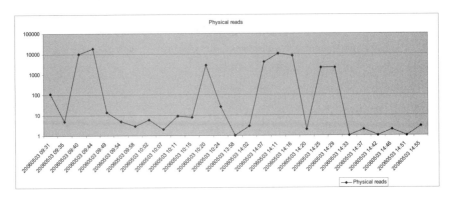

**Figure 3.18:** *Physical reads*

Figure 3.18 reveals that the system is performing very few physical reads, with peaks of around 10,000 physical reads over a 5 minute interval. This is less than 35 per second as there are 300 seconds in 5 minutes (5*60). To contrast this, the system was performing 27,000 logical I/Os per second at peak. But how are the I/Os being done, by table or by index reads?

Figure 3.19 shows this as it compares scattered reads verses sequential reads.

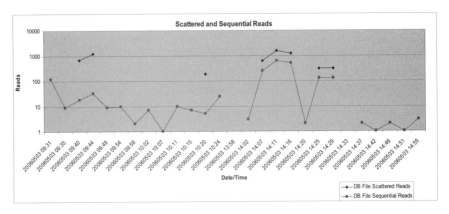

**Figure 3.19:** *Scattered and Sequential Reads*

As shown in Figure 3.19, sequential (index) reads are the predominate activity at the physical read level with only small periods of scattered reads.

The Issues queries are performing primarily in memory which is why their performance is excellent (sub-second on the average). If this could be maintained for the production environment, at least as far as the database is concerned, performance for these queries would be optimal.

However, it is projected that with the addition of the requirement to allow searching for issues that the current user (i.e. a supervisor checking on his subordinates issues) has no role would increase the number of table entries by a factor of around 20. This would increase the size to nearly a gigabyte, driving up physical reads if the current database memory size is maintained.

If the system shifts from predominately logical reads to predominately physical reads to satisfy the queries, processing time could increase by up to a factor of 17 to 100 times.

Figure 3.20 shows the time currently spent performing physical I/O for scattered and sequential reads.

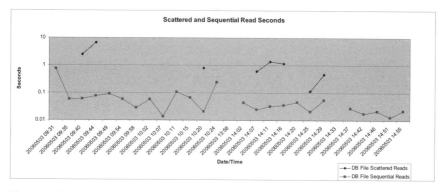

**Figure 3.20:** *Read Times*

Currently read times for sequential read activities are sub-second for a given interval, however if these were increased by a factor of 17, then the application would spend a much larger percentage of time in the physical I/O process, especially if scattered reads also increased as they are currently at the 1-10 second range when they occur.

Another way to look at physical I/O is via table scan rows and table rows by ROWID statistics. Figure 3.21 shows a comparison of these values.

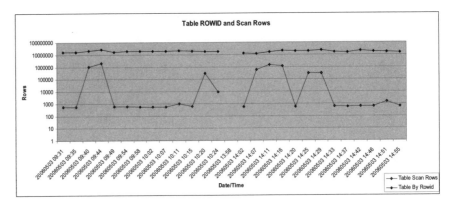

**Figure 3.21:** *Table scan and ROWID rows*

The graph in Figure 3.21 clearly shows the wide range between the index based reads and table scan based reads in the system.

## Operating System Activity

What about CPU and paging activity? Figure 3.22 shows the CPU activity representing one of the 78 user test runs.

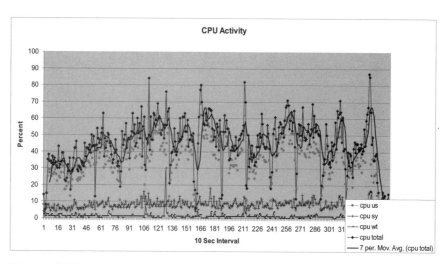

**Figure 3.22:** *CPU Activity*

In Figure 3.22 there appears to be a great number of processing peaks. These are due to the startup of the test users and can generally be disregarded. The 7 point moving average is a better indicator of actual CPU activity in this case and shows that even with 78 users hammering at the system, only 67 percent of CPU was reached. The issue that stopped testing at 78 users was memory related and not CPU.

Figure 3.23 shows memory usage as a function of time for the test period. Looking at the source data, the free memory dropped from 343 megabytes to 66 megabytes during the test period, about 3.5 megabytes of memory per user.

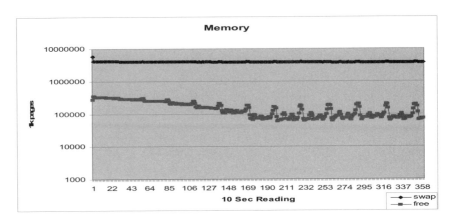

**Figure 3.23:** *Memory Usage*

Figure 3.24 shows system paging activity. As with the CPU activity there appears to be a great deal of spiking. This spiking in paging corresponds with the startup and release of the users during the test activity. Once the peaks are removed the overall system paging is well within expected ranges and is not a performance issue.

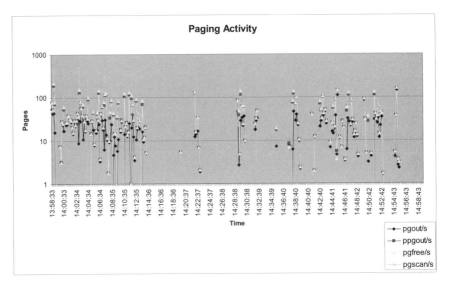

**Figure 3.24:** *Paging activity*

## Phase 1 Conclusion

Phase 1 shows that for the current data size (42 megabytes in the ISSUES base table) the data is completely cached in the database buffer area leading to excellent query performance at the database level. However, if system data volume increase by a factor of 20 as is predicted, then the memory will no longer be able to fully cache the ISSUES data and increased physical reads will seriously impact performance of the Issues queries.

Should the data size increase by a factor of 20, to get the same performance the database cache area would also need to be increased by a similar amount (from 500 megabytes to 10 gigabytes) unless some form of partitioning on the ISSUES table is utilized to reduce the working data set size.

In addition, increasing the data set size will increase the amount of logical I/O and CPU usage. If CPU usage increases by a factor of 20 due to increases in data set size, then to support the same 78 users with the same level of performance 10 CPUs would be required.

Using ratios the current configuration utilizes 0.87 percent of the available CPUs, (2) for each user at peak load, 68 percent of CPU at 78 users. Increasing the workload by a factor of 20 would drive CPU usage to 1740 percent, allowing that this is for 2 CPUs, each CPU would be doing 870 percent. Thus, at least 9 CPUs, assuming the data is fully cached, would be required to just handle the Issues type queries at a 78 user load with a factor of 20 data size increase.

# Maintaining Service Level Agreements (SLA's)

A Service Level Agreement (SLA) is a contractual agreement usually between a service provider such as a hosting service, and a client. However, SLA's have also been utilized between other departments and the IT department. Generally SLA's related to databases call for a specific response time. For example, a particular screen may need to be populated within 7 seconds or a particular report must return results within 3 seconds.

So how can the IT department ensure that it meets its specific SLA requirements? The IT department must define specific tests that are performed at specific intervals to verify SLA compliance, or lack of compliance, before the users notice. The results from the SLA performance tests are graphed or trended.

## Determining SLA Test Queries

Sometimes it will be easy to determine the query or queries to test for performance. For example, if a particular screen or report is the basis of the SLA, then the queries that fill the screen with data or the query that pulls the data for the report can be used to test for performance. However, it may not be that easy.

In previous sections of this chapter queries were presented that responded with data in sub-second response times, yet the application response time was over the SLA threshold of 3 seconds. The problem in the system in the previous section was the downstream reporting system. Even though the database responded in sub-second time, the downstream reporting system and web server resulted in delays that caused what the user saw as response time to be longer than the 3 second SLA threshold. It's a good idea to make sure the SLA threshold is just for items that can be controlled!

Must make sure that an SLA is meaningful for the specified part of the system and that the SLA specifies performance at each level of the system. So instead of just "must respond within 3 seconds to a user request," the SLA should read, "The database will respond to user generated SQL at the reporting layer interface within 3 seconds." What if the system with the 3 second SLA also had to service clients in Asia from a server in the Midwestern portion of the USA where the network latency was 500 milliseconds for each leg of the network round trip? Obviously whoever thought up the 3 second response SLA requirement did not work out the details of their own architecture, and whoever accepted such an SLA as a contractual obligation did not think about the full implications of the agreement.

SLAs should be meaningful and the queries tested should be of sufficient complexity and quantity to fully test the important parts of the SLA.

## Ok, here is the SLA and Queries, What Now?

Once a properly defined SLA and the queries to test it are in place, periodic testing routines that verify the SLA timing criteria are met must be set up. The tests must be run not just during off hours with a low load, but also during peak loads. After all, users obviously use the system during on-peak times as well as off-peak times.

Test scripts can be as simple as an SQL test harness routine that utilizes the pre-chosen SQL and is run periodically during the day to a mini-benchmark that is automatically run on a scheduled basis.

### Issues with Generating Your Own Scripts

If generating one's own SQL test harness, the following issues may develop:

- SQL may change, requiring recoding.

- It is very difficult to randomize code variables.

- Capturing timing values can be problematic.

Without a benchmark utility, the administrator is limited to either manually running the scripts and capturing the timings to verify the SLA, or developing an SQL test harness to inject code into the database. However, if the same SQL statements are injected in each test run, artificially good performances results may be achieved due to caching at the database level. Randomness must be introduced into SQL variables and queries must be run multiple times, then average the outcome to get valid results.

The pseudo-code for such an SQL test harness would look something like Figure 3.25.

```
Open procedure with "X" (number of times for each SQL iteration)
Loop 1: Choose Template SQL statement from SQL table
Loop 2: SQL Processing (iterate X times)
Read example SQL string from test SQL table
    Parse variables from code
    Loop3
            Read variable types and random values from variable
table
            Replace variables in SQL string with proper variable
    End Loop3
    Capture start timing
    Execute parsed and variable loaded SQL into cursor
    Capture end timing
    Calculate total time spent executing
        Load result table for executed SQL with timing
    End Loop2
End Loop 1
Calculate Averages for all SQL
Compare calculated averages to SLAs
Send alert if any SLA exceeded
End Procedure
```

**Figure 3.25:** *Pseudo-Code for SQL Test Harness*

In the procedure shown in Figure 3.25, three support tables are needed and some method of randomizing the values inserted into the test SQL must be utilized.

Once the procedure for executing and testing SQL is created, simply schedule it using *dbms_job*, the Oracle scheduler, cron, or whatever scheduler is used in the database.

## The Easy Way

If Oracle is being used, the Grid Control and Database Control interfaces allow database professionals to enter new procedures to calculate metrics which will be tested. The results can generate server alerts that will send administrator emails when SLAs are exceeded.

Another easy method is to use a Benchmark tool that allows administrators to enter the test SQL and program randomization of variables. The most difficult part is scheduling the test to run. Tools like Benchmark Factory will also email the results from SQL testing.

# Supporting Server & Storage Consolidations

Things always seem to move in waves, first something is up then it is down. In the beginning of the computer era everything was run on a single large machine; the mainframe, located in the "glass house," a sealed, air conditioned room. A lab-coated elite took user requests, and sometime in the future an answer would be received.

Then the people took the power and dared to have computers on their desktops. Each department insisted on their own servers, their own DBAs, their own support staff. This was the golden age of computers as far as consultants were concerned. Then came the budget crunches, and lo and behold everyone started passing their applications back to a central group for management.

This pushing of the applications to a central group has lead to the server and storage consolidation efforts. However, how can the database professional determine how many CPUS and how many gigabytes of memory are needed to support a consolidation of many applications onto a single large SMP computer? In addition to simple things such as number and speed of the CPUs, speed of memory needs considered as well as front side buses.

The number of needed CPUs can be quickly calculated by using the number of processing cycles available per CPU in the existing machines, times the number of processors times the peak percent busy. Summing the results and then using that with simple ratios to determine the number of new CPUs needed to meet the required cycle usage. A simple table such as the one shown in Figure 3.26 allows this calculation to be done easily.

| CPU Count Calculation | | | | | |
|---|---|---|---|---|---|
| CPU Count | Ghz | Peak % Busy | Raw | Hyperthreading | Equiv |
| 2 | 3 | 60 | 3.6 | Y | 6 |
| 1 | 2.7 | 70 | 1.89 | Y | 3 |
| 4 | 1.5 | 40 | 2.4 | N | 3 |
| 8 | 0.8 | 78 | 4.992 | N | 5 |
| | | | 0 | | 0 |
| | | | 0 | | 0 |
| | | | 0 | | 0 |
| | | | 0 | | 0 |
| | | | 0 | | 0 |
| | | | 0 | | 0 |
| | | | 0 | | 0 |
| | | | 0 | | 0 |
| | | | 0 | | 0 |
| | | | 0 | | 0 |

| CPU Count Calculation | | | | | | |
|---|---|---|---|---|---|---|
| Total/Avg: | 15 | 2 | 62 | 18.6 | | 17 |
| | Desired Ghz: | 3.2 | | | Needed CPUs: | 22 |
| | Peak Busy: | 30 | | | | |

**Figure 3.26:** *Example CPU Calculation Spreadsheet*

The calculations used in the spreadsheet cells are shown in Table 3.4.

| Column | Calculation |
|---|---|
| Raw | =B3*C3*(D3/100) |
| Equiv | =CEILING(IF((F3 = "Y"),E3*1.5,E3),1) |
| Needed CPUs | =CEILING(((D17*G17)/C20)*C17/C19,1) |

**Table 3.4:** *CPU Count Calculations*

Determining memory needs is a matter of looking at current usage during peak times across the various platforms to be consolidated and adding the results. Salesmen will run the line "faster memory means less memory, and faster CPUs mean less CPUs." Situations where clients bought into this "less is more" hype usually regretted it and ended up adding CPU and memory.

Determining disk needs can be much easier than determining the CPUs and memory needs. However, disk capacity is not the only variable that must be looked at, I/O capacity must be considered as well as user concurrency issues. Specify the disk array based on data size alone and the result will likely be poor performance. Always look at I/O rates and concurrency needs first, and allow no more than 90 I/O/sec per drive or less if using RAID5.

Concurrency is a bit harder to figure out, but if I/O rates are correct, concurrency will be pretty close as well.

The RAID calculations for RAID10 and RAID5 are shown in the spreadsheet in Figure 3.27. The example is for I/O to a single Oracle instance but simply combining the results from multiple spreadsheets should present a good starting point for sizing a combined system.

RAID ARRAY CALCULATIONS

| Instance: | TO1P | | RAID01 factor: | 0.82 | RAID5 Factor: | 0.62 | RAID5 Write Penalty: | 1.3 |
|---|---|---|---|---|---|---|---|---|
| Meas. Dur: | 1 | | # Mirrors: | 2 | DISK IO Rate: | 200 | | |

| Mount Point | Physical Reads | Physical Writes | Sum Reads+ Writes | IO/sec | RAID01 NMR | RAID01 MR | RAID5 | RAID5 Adjusted IO | RAID5 IO rate |
|---|---|---|---|---|---|---|---|---|---|
| 1 | 800 | 200.00 | 1,000.00 | 1,000.00 | 14 | 8 | 10 | 1,060.00 | 1,060.00 |
| | | | 0.00 | 0.00 | 0 | 0 | 3 | 0.00 | 0.00 |
| | | | 0.00 | 0.00 | 0 | 0 | 3 | 0.00 | 0.00 |
| | | | 0.00 | 0.00 | 0 | 0 | 3 | 0.00 | 0.00 |
| | | | 0.00 | 0.00 | 0 | 0 | 3 | 0.00 | 0.00 |
| | | | 0.00 | 0.00 | 0 | 0 | 3 | 0.00 | 0.00 |
| | | | 0.00 | 0.00 | 0 | 0 | 3 | 0.00 | 0.00 |
| | | | 0.00 | 0.00 | 0 | 0 | 3 | 0.00 | 0.00 |
| | | | 0.00 | 0.00 | 0 | 0 | 3 | 0.00 | 0.00 |
| | | | 0.00 | 0.00 | 0 | 0 | 3 | 0.00 | 0.00 |
| | | | 0.00 | 0.00 | 0 | 0 | 3 | 0.00 | 0.00 |
| | | | 0.00 | 0.00 | 0 | 0 | 3 | 0.00 | 0.00 |
| Totals | 800.00 | 200.00 | 1,000.00 | 1,000.00 | 14 | 8 | 10 | 1,060.00 | 1,060.00 |

| | Label (For entered value) |
|---|---|
| Variable | Manual Entry |
| | Title |
| | Calculated Values |
| Constant | Default (can be changed) |
| RAID01 NMR | RAID01 No Multi-Read |

| RAID ARRAY CALCULATIONS |
| --- |
| RAID01 MR    RAID01 Multi-Read Capable |
| RADI01 Factor based on 90/110 with 90 being best observed rate |
| RAID5 Factor based on RAID01 factor less 25% for RAID5 IO penalties (1*0.82-(0.82*0.25)) |
| RAID5 is also more costly the more WRITE activity so a write penalty of 5 (which is low based on experience) is also assessed. |
| Number of Mirrors currently works for just 2, haven't figured out a complex enough formula for the other levels. |
| Minimum number of RAID10 disks figured to be 2 or a multiple of 2, if less than 4 RAID0 is assumed. |
| Minimum number of RAID5 drives assumed to be 3 (2 data and one equivalent for parity data) |

**Figure 3.27:** *Example Disk Calculations*

Using the above techniques one should be able to get fairly close to the needed amount of memory and CPUs for consolidated server, as well as the number of disks.

# Conclusion

In this chapter, the uses of benchmark tools to perform capacity analysis and prediction have been examined. Examples were shown using the Quest Benchmark Factory tool to demonstrate the use of such tools for trending and planning for future needs.

The use of manual tools, such as spreadsheets, to do predictions of needed CPUs, memory, and disks in server consolidations were also included in this chapter.

In the next chapter, the use of tools to perform stress testing of databases will be covered.

# Stressing the Database

## Introduction

Benchmarking has a simple purpose – to mitigate the huge risks introduced when an expensive, large-scale, or mission-critical application goes into production by identifying performance bottlenecks. Benchmarking the behavior of a database minimizes this risk. However, a benchmark is only effective if it properly informs your decision making. Do you have enough CPU power? Is there enough memory? Can your I/O subsystem handle the expected load and, for that matter, how much more can it handle above the expected load? The only way to receive answers to these questions, and more, is by stress testing the database.

# Database Implosion Therapy

The common connotation for the word 'implosion' is a process in which objects are destroyed by collapsing in on themselves. Psychiatry has an interesting concept called "implosion therapy". It is described by this definition:

Implosion therapy - a technique used in behavioral therapy where the client is flooded with experiences of a particular kind until becoming either averse to them or numbed to them.

In a sense, by benchmarking the database and application we are attempting a form of implosion therapy. The idea is to 'flood' the components of the application with so many high-activity transactions that their performance either bottlenecks (i.e. causes the performance of the test environment to plateau and possibly even crash) or shows more ability to scale.

To achieve a high confidence in database stress tests, we require clearly defined assumptions. Generally, database stress tests work under the assumption that we know what are:

- Acceptable response times for the database server.

- Expected user and/or connection loads to the database server.

Once the assumptions are set, we are ready to define the database stress test in a cycle of:

- Run stress/implosion test
- Record and measure performance
- Performance tune the database
- Repeat until:
  - The database achieves the expected level of performance, thereby setting the baseline configuration for the database.
  - The database's upper limit for performance is ascertained, thereby setting the performance high watermark for the database.

Stress testing may or may not be iterative. For example, stress testing may be used as a means of establishing a new baseline for future benchmark tests.

The stress testing process follows a simple plan. Load on the database, both in terms of connections and the number of transactions, continually ramp up until the database is no longer responsive at an acceptable level. Performance indicators are then measured and recorded, results are analyzed and interpreted, and as a result, either expectations are scaled back or performance is tuned. Remember, it is time for tuning when the database has failed to meet the required minimum levels of performance on the given OS- and hardware configurations.

## Hardware Issues in Stress Testing

Stress testing today's database servers is not as easy as it used to be. The state of the art for hardware has continued to advance dramatically. So a benchmarking test that would have stressed a database server well beyond the breaking point five years ago will not cause a current server to even skip a beat. That means it actually takes a lot of thought in designing benchmark tests to get a truly representative workload that properly stresses the server.

Here is an example comparing the hardware and benchmarking issues of the older style "WinTel" hardware and the current generation of "WinTel" hardware. Older CPU architectures running Windows were entirely 32-bit (with the exception of DEC Alpha CPUs) and very predictably limited the amount of addressable memory available to the database, application, and operating system. On the other hand, 64-bit CPUs running Windows enable access to a vastly greater amount of memory. Consequently, a well-designed benchmark that may have thoroughly stressed even a three or four year old server by bottlenecking at memory would experience no problems in a 64-bit environment with much greater memory.

A more sophisticated and subtle example of some of the changes that have occurred between older and newer WinTel systems involves hyperthreaded CPUs on Windows Server and Microsoft SQL Server 2000 databases.

Shortly after hyperthreaded CPUs were shipped, customers began to notice that on high-end workloads with very heavy CPU utilization, the performance actually degraded with hyperthreaded CPUs rather than improved. Remember that hyperthreading promised improved CPU performance by allowing different elements of a processor to run different code simultaneously, thus boosting chip performance and allowing a hyperthreaded CPU to process much more information. Customers also noticed that the same CPUs saw slightly increased usage but better performance with hyperthreading enabled. So what was the culprit and how could benchmarking have helped?

The root cause of the problem is that hyperthreading forces two *logical* processors to share the L1 and L2 caches of a single *physical* processor. So whenever SQL Server ran an extremely memory intensive thread on one of the logical CPUs that consumed all of the physical L1 and/or L2 cache, such as lazywriter or a very demanding worker thread, then threads running on the other logical CPU would be starved for cache. In some cases, the cache starvation could cause the worker thread to wait on a spinlock. The resulting loss of available cache and possibility of spinlocks caused customers to see a slowdown on hyperthreading-enable servers. Disabling hyperthreading on the CPUs, in general, contributed a 10% improvement in performance.

Interestingly, though, some applications running against the very same hardware with hyperthreading-enabled did see a performance gain. How so? In those cases, the application usually had very small, compact SQL statements and procedural code (e.g. stored procedures and user-defined functions) that ran so quickly and so compactly as to not compete with the lazywriter regularly.

The point to this discussion is that stress tests are not static. A stress test built three years ago will almost certainly be insufficient today. The best way to stress a database is to build an application workload that is as close to "real world" as possible. If the database will be used strictly for OLTP applications, then the workload should contain many INSERT, UPDATE, DELETE, and SELECT statements. If the database will be used for BI applications, then the workload should contain many realistic, complex queries that truly tax the system just as the actual users would. Any test workload that is less than realistic should be assumed to be biased, which must be taken into account when interpreting the results of the benchmarks.

## Configuring the Server Environment

The ability to stress test the database in an environment that is identical to the production server environment is the ideal.

However, it is a common difficulty in stress testing specialized environments that it may not be affordable or convenient to reproduce the production server configuration in its entirety. In cases like that, it is a good idea to create a staging environment which is a more affordable or configurable subset of the production environment. In a situation like this, it is best to assess the difference in performance capabilities between the test and production environments and then factor those differences into the final analysis of the stress test(s).

Further concepts around hardware and configuring the server environment are discussed in Chapter 5: Preparing the Benchmark.

## Stress Testing Specific Workloads

As described earlier, the stress test must be characterized by its most basic assumptions, then further categorized and sorted by:

- workloads:
  - read-only stress testing
  - transactional stress testing, also known as DML stress testing or OLTP (on-line transaction processing) stress testing
- tasks, for example:
  - backups
  - recovery
  - data loading
  - data exports
- functional areas, such as inventory or sales

- business processes, such as closing the monthly or quarterly accounting period

It also makes sense to further divide the top-level workload into smaller and more manageable testing packages that contain a good representative user mix. Stress testing an OLTP workload scaling up to 1000 concurrent users is a good example of this. But it may better enable the database professional to test the system by having a mix of 100 concurrent user packages that can be mixed and matched in stress test runs.

Building test packages for read-only or OLTP stress tests is most easily performed by recording the SQL statements executed during a given time period. The time periods recorded should contain a representative mix of users and transactions. The time periods may also reflect a specific set of activities, such as the batch process that consumes the most resources or the busiest hours of a typical business day. Once recorded, all of the transactions (SELECT, INSERT, UPDATE, and DELETE statements) and stored procedure calls become the source of the replayed workload.

It is vital to capture a reasonable workload of important batch processes too. For example, many database systems schedule activities such as backups and data imports and exports during non-peak hours, such as the evenings when most employees are at home. Batch processes workload should be recorded as well for a full understanding of the behavior of the database during stress testing.

When using Quest Software's Benchmark Factory tool, it is advisable to use the potent record and playback tools that ship with each database platform. After all, reproducing real users acting upon a replica of the production database is the best means of determining bottlenecks and estimating future performance. Oracle provides several different methods for creating a trace file, such as the DBMS_SUPPORT and DBMS_MONITOR packages, as well as tools like SQL*Trace. Microsoft SQL Server provides tracing through SQL Profiler and through several system stored procedures that enable server-side tracing of client activities. In Oracle, production activity can be recorded in a trace file through the ALTER SYSTEM/SESSION SET EVENTS '10046 trace name context forever, level 4' (level 4 or above records bind variable values) and then replayed in Benchmark Factory.

By using this approach to test a database, much time and money can be saved when the other tiers of application do not have to be stress tested and when full-blown end-to-end stress testing is not a requirement.

## Stressing Read-Only Databases (Read-only Implosion)

Read-Only or Read-Intensive databases are most common in Business Intelligence (BI) applications. Typically, databases used for BI contain vast amounts of data and may even have complex "star" or "snowflake" schemas that facilitate aggregation of data for reporting purposes. Consequently, building a stress test that can achieve read-only implosion on a BI database requires lots of queries, some of which may be very complex and span many tables.

Read-only stress testing can reveal bottlenecks in a variety of different areas on both Oracle and SQL Server. Some common bottlenecks revealed during stressing read-only databases include:

- Poorly cached or inadequate number of cached execution plans

- Blocking

- Full-table and full-index table scans

- Poor indexing strategy

- Poor SQL statement construction, such as poor search arguments for WHERE clauses or heavy overhead from HAVING clauses

- Disk I/O limitations on the disk subsystem, especially in temporary workspaces such as the TEMPD database on Microsoft SQL Server

Benchmark Factory includes several pre-defined benchmarks to ease stress testing setup and configuration, including the TPC-H benchmark. TPC-H is a read-intensive benchmark, created by the Transaction Processing Counsel (http://www.tpc.org). It consists of a pre-defined database schema with data and a suite of business-oriented queries and concurrent transactions that analyze large volumes of data, issue highly complex queries, and answer critical business questions through reporting queries.

The TPC-H benchmark supplants the older TPC-D read-intensive benchmark. However, Benchmark Factory also offers the older TPC-D benchmark. TPC-H reports a performance metric and is called the Composite Query-per-Hour Performance Metric (OphH@Size). It represents the multiple capabilities of the system to process queries, both on a single stream and on multiple concurrent users.

The following example shows a 100 user TPC-H benchmark test run on a Tecra T41 with 1.5gb of RAM and a single 80gb hard disk. As shown in Table 4.1, the Tecra TPC-H test ran slowly. To fully stress the system using the TCP-H read-intensive workload, simply scale the number of users until the system became non-responsive. Chapter 6: Running the Benchmark, fully describes the process of setting up and running a test using Benchmark Factory.

| Name | Rows | Bytes | Avg Trans Time | Avg Interarrival Time | Avg Response Time |
|---|---|---|---|---|---|
| Promotion Effect Query (Q14) | 1 | 8 | 301.746 | 0.000 | 301.746 |
| Minimum Cost Supplier Query (Q2) | 480 | 116640 | 30.650 | 0.000 | 30.593 |
| Product Type Profit Measure Query (Q9) | 175 | 6475 | 672.282 | 0.000 | 672.282 |
| Potential Part Promotion Query (Q20) | 0 | 0 | 10.910 | 0.000 | 10.910 |
| Forecasting Revenue Change Query (Q6) | 1 | 8 | 40.525 | 0.000 | 40.525 |
| Small-Quantity-Order Revenue Query (Q17) | 1 | 8 | 24.177 | 0.000 | 24.177 |
| Large Volume Customer Query (Q18) | 3 | 99 | 841.329 | 0.000 | 841.329 |
| National Market Share Query (Q8) | 2 | 24 | 356.418 | 0.000 | 356.418 |
| Suppliers Who Kept Orders Waiting Query (Q21) | 421 | 12209 | 885.663 | 0.000 | 885.655 |
| Customer Distribution Query (Q13) | 34 | 272 | 19.996 | 0.000 | 19.982 |
| Shipping Priority Query (Q3) | 80595 | 3143205 | 427.040 | 0.000 | 426.246 |
| Global Sales Opportunity Query (Q22) | 4 | 40 | 4.135 | 0.000 | 4.135 |
| Parts-Supplier Relationship Query (Q16) | 19607 | 843101 | 22.551 | 0.000 | 22.393 |
| Order Priority Checking Query (Q4) | 0 | 0 | 0.167 | 0.000 | 0.167 |

| | | | | | |
|---|---|---|---|---|---|
| Important Stock Identification Query (Q11) | 1089 | 13068 | 46.510 | 0.000 | 46.506 |
| Top Supplier Query (Q15) | 1 | 92 | 263.518 | 0.000 | 263.517 |
| Pricing Summary Report Query (Q1) | 0 | 0 | 0.159 | 0.000 | 0.159 |
| Returned Item Reporting Query (Q10) | 21914 | 5303188 | 348.999 | 0.000 | 348.370 |
| Discounted Revenue Query (Q19) | 1 | 8 | 401.972 | 0.000 | 401.955 |
| Local Supplier Volume Query (Q5) | 5 | 165 | 338.777 | 0.000 | 338.777 |
| Volume Shipping Query (Q7) | 4 | 248 | 358.608 | 0.000 | 358.608 |
| Shipping Modes and Order Priority Query (Q12) | 2 | 36 | 334.276 | 0.000 | 334.276 |

**Table 4.1:** *TPC-H Queries Processing Using Benchmark Factory*

# Stressing OLTP Databases (DML Implosion)

Relatively few databases are *only* OLTP-oriented. Even the most OLTP-oriented database will have lots of SELECT statements to perform lookups for various values. Nevertheless, the idea behind achieving DML implosion on an OLTP database is to ramp up the user load and number of INSERT, UPDATE, and DELETE statements in a mix that realistically reproduces the activity of human users until the database no longer performs adequately.

OLTP stress testing can reveal bottlenecks of their own sort. Some common bottlenecks revealed during stressing OLTP databases include:

- Locking issues

- Record and table blocking

- Poor indexing strategy, including inadequate PCTFREE on Oracle or inadequate FILL_FACTOR on SQL Server

- Poor SQL statement construction

- Disk I/O limitations on the disk subsystem, including possible opportunities for partitioning

Benchmark Factory also includes a couple of pre-defined benchmarks specifically for OLTP stress testing, AS3AP and TCP-B.

The AS3AP benchmark was created by the American National Standards Institute (ANSI) as an SQL relational database benchmark. It is a good general purpose benchmarking test for a single database server all the way up to a high-performance parallel processing machine or a distributed database system.

Benchmark Factory ships with the TPC-C. It is probably the most popular database benchmark and OLTP stress test on the market today and is frequently updated by the TPC to keep it current with the best practices of the day. TPC-C consists of a pre-defined database schema with data and a suite of business-oriented concurrent transactions that creates, removes, modifies, and queries data.

For example, a 100 user TPC-C benchmark test ran rather quickly on a Tecra T41 with 1.5gb of RAM and a single 80gb hard disk. As shown in Figure 4.1, the Tecra could easily handle 100 users. To fully stress the system using the TCP-C OLTP workload, simply scale the number of users until the system became non-responsive. Chapter 6: Running the Benchmark, fully describes the process of setting up and running a test using Benchmark Factory.

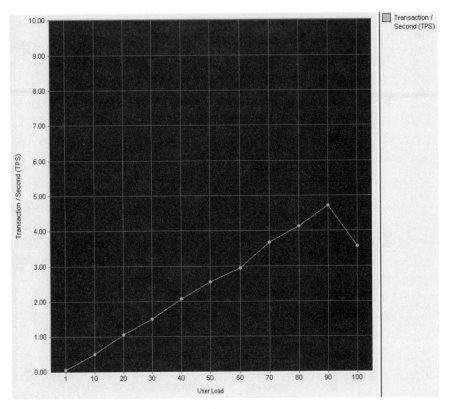

**Figure 4.1:** *TPC-C Transactions/Sec per 10 users*

In case of Figure 4.1, the OLTP workload and the database's general responsiveness scaled linearly. To complete the stress test, the Benchmark Factory would be used to scale the test to the point of unresponsiveness. The performance of the database and its underlying hardware would then be assessed to determine if the configuration met the user's needs.

If not, the system could be tuned and then retested. If so, the user would have a strong assurance that the current hardware, database, and software configuration was adequate.

## Stressing Mixed Databases (General Implosion)

The most common sort of database applications run with a mix of simple reads (SELECT statements performing value lookups), complex reads (SELECT statements running reports and performing BI), and business transactions (INSERT, UPDATE, and DELETE statements).

There are a few key behaviors that must be rigorously controlled during a general implosion stress test:

- The number of test iterations.

- The ramp up of concurrent users and/or worker threads.

- The mix of SELECT, INSERT, UPDATE, and DELETE statements.

The mixed database stress test is the type described throughout the remainder of this book. Refer to Chapter 6 for more details.

# Stressing Specialized Environments

The previous section described the importance of building benchmarks that effectively stress test the database according to the type of workload expected on the database: read-only, OLTP, or mixed.

However, there are other types of specialized environments that have a major impact on the way the database professional will perform database benchmarking. In this case, three types of environments – distributed systems, consolidated systems, and virtual systems will be investigated. Remember that the goal of benchmarking is to identify and eliminate bottlenecks.

# Stressing Distributed Systems

Stress testing a distributed database system injects several added layers of complexity and opportunities for failure into the mix. Take, for example, a multi-tiered application with clients connecting to a web application that connects back to multiple database servers that replicate data amongst each other.

To properly stress the database supporting an application of this type, we must assess the possibility of bottlenecks at multiple levels including:

- at the **application level**: by monitoring the end-user experience for roundtrip transaction times.

- at the **database level**: by monitoring all of the regular performance indicators measured during read-only, OLTP, or mixed usage databases.

- at the **mid-tier level**: by measuring connection trafficking, transaction throughput, and other performance indicators, we can determine the acceptable performance of the mid-tier server(s) under load.

- at the **operating system level**: by tracking OS-level metrics such as CPU consumption, memory, disk I/O, and so forth.

- at the **network level**: by assessing the latency of replication activities, the utilization of the network and ports, and looking for bottlenecks throughout the replicated environment.

In our case, we are primarily interested in stress testing distributed database systems. In this scenario, you must modify your stress test in the following ways:

- Begin with a clearly defined workload test of the types described earlier (read-only, OLTP, or mixed).

- Perform the workload stress test on a non-distributed configuration, if possible. The results of this test give a good baseline to compare the results of the same test when fully distributed.

- Isolate and compartmentalize the stress test workload sufficiently so that all databases in the mix can be stress tested.

  - For example, assume that you have a centralized database server that replicates summarized data out to the field office database servers. Meanwhile, the field office database servers are busily processing the OLTP workload generated by the employees in that field office. Consequently, you should have a hardware environment that reproduces this production environment and a database workload that can stress each of the field servers in your text plus the central office server.

  - Another example is to setup and configure an Oracle RAC environment. An example of this exact scenario is found in Chapter 6.

- Monitor the interaction of the databases in the distributed system.

- Compile and assess the results of stress tests holistically by including all components of the test.

## Stressing Consolidated Systems

Stress testing consolidated database systems presents issues that are, in many ways, the inverse of those presented by testing a distributed system. Distributed systems are usually deployed for one of two reasons. First, distributed systems are deployed to localize processing activity at a local business site. Second, distributed systems are deployed to share the database workload across many servers, thereby lessening the load on any single server.

When an IT organization decides to consolidate databases, its reason is usually to improve maintainability and reliability while lowering costs by locating the hardware and software at a centralized center of excellence, such as the corporate IT headquarters. Another common reason for consolidating databases is to take advantage of new, high-performance hardware that can easily accommodate the load of many older, obsolete servers. For example, many organizations are consolidating their older, 32-bit Windows database servers onto much larger and more powerful 64-bit Windows database servers.

To accommodate a database stress test for a consolidated database system, you should:

- Begin with a clearly defined workload test of the types described earlier (read-only, OLTP, or mixed). Ideally, you should use the current workload of database server being considered for consolidation by recording the workload activities using one of the platform specific tools mentioned earlier in this chapter.

- Perform the workload stress test on the older configuration, if possible. The results of this test give a good baseline to compare the results of the same test when fully consolidated. You should be able to clearly identify the ROI and delta of performance between the old distributed configuration and the new consolidated configuration.

- Isolate and compartmentalize the stress test workload sufficiently so that all databases in the mix can be stress tested. For example, Microsoft SQL Servers can support many distinct databases, each associated with their own consolidated application. Will hosting a variety of databases on a single, high-end, consolidated server interfere too much with each other or not?

- Monitor the interaction of the databases in the consolidated system.

- Compile and assess the results of stress tests holistically by including all components of the test.

## Stressing Virtualized Systems

Stressing virtualized systems may be undertaken from a couple standpoints. First, you can stress test an individual, virtualized database on the host server and track only the performance of the virtualized database. Second, you can stress test the host server, stressing one or more of the virtual servers on the host, and monitoring the specific behavior of the database of greatest interest.

A key factor to remember in constructing and running a stress test is to keep the test as simple as possible while ensuring that the results are dependable and reliable for good decision making. Thus, if you can reasonably assure the performance of the database without stress testing the entire virtual server host, then you should do so.

If, however, you are not certain what impact other virtual servers hosted on the same physical server will have, then you should test the entire virtual server host. That can make matters much more complicated because you will have to build a replayable workload not only for the database that you are most interested in testing, but also for all activities that occur on the virtual server host.

To accommodate a database stress test for a virtualized database system, you should:

- Begin with a clearly defined workload test of the types described earlier (read-only, OLTP, or mixed).

- Perform the workload stress test against the virtual database server. Meanwhile, collect overall system utilization metrics so that performance of the virtual database can always be correlated against the overall resource utilization on the server.

- Isolate and compartmentalize the stress test workload sufficiently so that all virtual databases on the hosting server if more than one database exists on the server can be stress tested.

- Monitor the interaction of the databases with the virtual server host.

- Compile and assess the results of stress tests holistically by including all components of the test, such as other virtual servers on the host.

## Stressing Specific Database Platforms

In some cases, it may be necessary to stress test a database *platform* and compare the results to determine which of the Oracle or Microsoft SQL Server platforms will offer better performance, reliability, scalability, or maintainability compared to the other. Perhaps the issue is the cost of the hardware, OS, and database software to their relative processing powers. In any of these cases, great care must be taken to ensure that the stress test workloads are *interoperable* among the various database platforms being tested or else the results may be very badly skewed.

As with previous sections in this chapter, the more realistic a workload that can be provided for the stress test, the better information you will receive for decision making. However, every database platform has its own peculiarities and quirks that make it distinct and different from others. Therefore, an application written for a single platform may, in fact, work well *only* on that platform not because other platforms are bad, but because the application can only take advantage of the features of its "native" database platform. The following sections describe a few quick caveats to remember when stress testing a workload that may not have been designed for interoperability on other database platforms.

## Not all SQL Implementations up to Spec

The ANSI SQL standard is extremely popular both for the IT community and for the database platform vendors who support the community. But just because database platform vendors and their users really like the ANSI SQL standard does not mean that they have implemented all aspects of the standard.

Note: the TCP benchmark tests are all ANSI SQL standard and will run without modification on both Oracle and Microsoft SQL Server.

Additionally, all of the database platform vendors are in a sort of competitive foot race to provide better features and capabilities to the community. Meanwhile, the ANSI SQL standards committee meets and revises the standard at its own pace. It is therefore not uncommon to see a database platform vendor who offers a feature within their implementation of the SQL language that is not in the ANSI SQL standard at all. In other cases, the ANSI SQL standards are updated to include a feature already supported by a database platform vendor, but given a unique and conflicting name to that used by the vendor.

There is an example from Chapter 3 that describes some capacity planning steps involving a materialized view on an Oracle database. The term 'materialized view', meaning a view that actually has its own data that is physically separate from the base tables, is supported by the ANSI SQL standard. If the same script was run on Microsoft SQL Server, the script would fail when it tried to create a materialized view. Does that mean that SQL Server does not support the feature desired? No – SQL Server does, in fact, support an 'instantiated view' structure but it calls them an indexed view rather than a materialized view.

Oracle has its own procedural extensions to the ANSI SQL standard called PL/SQL, used to write stored procedures, user-defined functions, and the like. PL/SQL is not part of ANSI SQL. Similarly, Microsoft SQL Server has its own procedural language called Transact-SQL. Anything written in Transact-SQL is not supported by the ANSI standard and would not run on an Oracle database.

Each database platform vendor supports transaction *hints* that tell the database query optimizer how to process a given query. For example, a hint could be used to specify which index the query optimizer is to use. Optimizer hints are entirely database specific, are not supported under the ANSI SQL standard, and should not be expected to be interoperable among database platforms.

Each of the database platform vendors maintains copious syntax and statement information about their implementations of the ANSI SQL standard. A full examination of those differences would be quite lengthy here.

The key lesson to remember is that vendor documentation should always be examined to understand what elements of the transactions and, if present, procedural code is interoperable on other database platforms. You may have to make significant changes to your workloads if they are to be tested on more than one database platform, unless SQL code has been written to the lowest common denominator among the various database platforms.

## Not all Query Optimizers Created Equal

It almost goes without saying that some queries run faster (or slower) when run on various database platforms due to various low-level architectural differences in the database platforms. For example, MySQL received a strong reputation as being an extremely fast database platform for running a SQL-based website application. The only downside to that reputation was the MySQL did not do 'ACID' transactions, meaning that neither an ANSI SQL standard COMMIT nor ROLLBACK command could be issued. So you would certainly get much faster performance if you never worried about whether you could recover from the effect of any specific transaction.

Here is a specific example comparing Oracle and Microsoft SQL Server. Oracle uses cursors, behind the scenes, to implement any standard ad-hoc SELECT statement. Therefore, a query issued against an Oracle database through either a cursor or a SELECT statement will have essentially the same performance profile. It will run in about the same amount of time, consume the same amount of memory, and issue the same sort of lock.

Microsoft SQL Server, however, uses different low-level structures for SELECT statements and for cursors. Cursors consume their own space in memory and, when completed, must be manually deallocated from the memory space. Therefore, on Microsoft SQL Server, a cursor-based query will perform more slowly, acquire locks differently, and use a different (and usually greater) amount of memory than a query issued through a SELECT statement.

So if a cursor-rich workload is moved from Oracle to a Microsoft SQL Server, the Microsoft SQL Server would perform slower. The Microsoft SQL Server would gradually lose memory as cursors were created, but their memory would not be deallocated when they were done. If the same Oracle workload containing only SELECT-based queries were moved, there would be no significant difference in the underlying architecture between the query optimization approaches used by the two database platforms.

## Conclusion

The steps required to construct a valid stress test follow a simple mantra — repeatable, deconstructable, and well-defined. This chapter has described the assumptions needed to begin designing a stress test. Some hardware and configuration issues were highlighted. Three specific stress-testing workloads and their related challenges were detailed: read-only, OLTP, and mixed.

This chapter also covered three important and specialized database environments and the challenges involved in stress testing them: distributed database systems, consolidated database systems, and virtual database systems. Finally, general tips were presented for dealing with creating interoperable, or at least database platform-agnostic, stress tests.

# Preparing for Benchmarking

# Isolate the Benchmark Environment

Benchmark results must be both reliable and repeatable in order to foster conclusions that are predictable and projectable. Thus an obvious requirement is that the benchmark hardware should be isolated from other production, development or test environments. Now that sounds easy enough, but in today's world of consolidated disk storage and consolidated servers, not to mention server virtualization, this may not be as intuitive as it seems.

Most people would make the clear choice to keep the application and database server standalone. And some might even go so far as to place the benchmark environment on its own network segment – although with today's high speed gigabit and faster networks, that is probably not totally necessary anymore. But what about more complex hardware configurations such as shared storage and virtualized servers, where the definition of separation becomes somewhat more nebulous. Proponents of these new technologies may tell you that even though there are shared hardware resources, they are managed and maintained as totally separate – with little to no ability to affect each other.

The answer is really quite simple – there should be nothing shared in order to obtain reliable and repeatable test results. So benchmark environments should not utilize a shared storage device, such as a Storage Area Network (SAN) or Network Attached Storage (NAS), which is being currently used by any other application or database. Furthermore, the only virtualized server environment that one might consider would be to place clustered database nodes across virtual servers, so in essence, virtualization limited to offering servers for just a single database in order to lessen the possibility of skewed results.

# Prepare the Server Operating System

There are entire collections of books written on the subject of tuning and optimizing operating system performance. So it would be unreasonable to try to cover such a broad and exhaustive topic in this book. But nonetheless there are some major and important operating system settings to verify setting properly in order to obtain the most indicative results. The following two sections will cover several such settings for Windows and Linux.

## Windows

The Windows Registry is a very large and complex repository for numerous operating system, database and application configuration settings – many of which can affect performance to varying degrees.

- Enable a large size file system cache – This entry controls whether the system maintains a standard size or a large size file system cache. Enabling a larger cache makes sense for database servers with sufficient memory.

  - Key:
    HKEY_LOCAL_MACHINE\System\CurrentControlSet \ Control\Session Manager\Memory Management

  - Data type: REG_DWORD

  - Value to set: 1

- Disable paging of the kernel code - This entry controls whether the user and kernel mode drivers and the kernel mode core system code itself can be paged. Disabling the paging of kernel code makes sense for database servers with sufficient memory.

- Key:
  HKEY_LOCAL_MACHINE\System\CurrentControlSet
  \ Control\Session Manager\Memory Management

- Data type: REG_DWORD

- Value to set: 1

- I/O Page Lock Limit - This entry controls the maximum amount of RAM that can be locked for I/O operations. The default minimizes RAM usage. An I/O intensive system could benefit from larger buffer sizes. Caution: setting this parameter too high can result in slower performance. Set it in increments and see how it affects the system.

  - Key:
    HKEY_LOCAL_MACHINE\System\CurrentControlSet
    \ Control\Session Manager\Memory Management

  - Data type: REG_DWORD

  - Value to set:
    - if RAM <= 32MB then IoPageLockLimit = 512
    - if RAM > 32MB then IoPageLockLimit = 4K
    - if RAM > 64MB then IoPageLockLimit = 8K
    - if RAM > 128MB then IoPageLockLimit = 16K
    - if RAM > 160MB then IoPageLockLimit = 32K
    - if RAM > 256MB then IoPageLockLimit = 64K

- Disable Last Access Update - When Windows accesses a directory or reads a file on an NTFS volume, it updates the "Last Access" time stamp. Disabling last access update will increase the speed of all disk I/O – as it will avoid updating access time every time.

- Key:
  HKEY_LOCAL_MACHINE\System\CurrentControlSet
  \ Control\FileSystem

- Data type: REG_DWORD

- Value to set: 1

- Diskperf – Most benchmarking on the Windows platform involves at least some use of Performance Monitor counters. However, Windows NT 4.0 disables all disk counters for Performance Monitor by default. Windows 2000 enables only the Physical Disk PerfMon object and disables the Logical Disk PerfMon object off by default. (Windows 2003 does a much better job of this by default.) This behavior can be manually controlled using the DISKPERF program at system startup. When enabled using the syntax DISKPERF –y, PerfMon records a timestamp on all physical and logical disk I/Os, tracking the time that the I/O starts and completes. "DISKPERF –yv" should be placed in the startup process on any benchmarking server. (Note that diskperf settings only take effect upon startup. If diskperf is run after the system has been up for a while, the system must be rebooted for it to take effect. Since diskperf does add some system overhead, it may be disabled for older or heavily stressed hardware – but *not* during benchmarking.) Other diskperf switches include:

  - –Y Tells the system to start both logical and physical disk performance counters when the computer is restarted.

  - -YD Enables the disk performance counters for only physical drives when the computer is restarted.

  - -YV Enables the disk performance counters for only logical drives or storage volumes when the computer is restarted.

  - -N Tells the system to disable all disk performance counters when the computer is restarted.

- -ND Disables the disk performance counters for only physical drives.

- -NV Disables the disk performance counters for only logical drives or storage volumes

## Linux

Unfortunately (or fortunately, depending upon your viewpoint) Linux does not have a single place whereby administrators can make all their operating system performance modifications. Here are three though worth taking the time and trouble to perform.

The first thing anyone should do to Linux after the install is to create a monolithic kernel (i.e. recompile the kernel to statically include libraries intend to be used and to turn off dynamically loaded modules). The idea is that a smaller kernel with just the features needed is superior to a fat kernel supporting things that are not needed. Now there are literally hundreds of parameters to set and a dozen good books or web sites to reference on the subject. Some key parameters that stick out in my mind include CPU type, SMP support, APIC support, DMA support, IDE DMA default enabled and quota support. Our advice, go through them all – and read the xconfig help if you are unsure. The actual steps are really quite simple:

- cd /usr/src/linux

- make mrproper

- make xconfig (setting all the options you wish to tune)

- make dep clean bzImage

- cp /usr/src/linux/arch/i386/boot/bzImage /boot/vmlinuz-kernel.version.number

- cp /usr/src/linux/System.map /boot/System.map.kernal.version.number

- edit boot configuration file to include new kernel

- lilo

- edit /etc/lilo.conf

- run lilo

- grub

- edit /etc/grub/grub.conf

- reboot

If everything has been done correctly, the machine will boot using the new, leaner and meaner kernel.

The second and often most productive Linux modification attempts to reduce unnecessary file I/O operations. By default, Linux updates the last time read attribute of any file during a read operation. It does this as well for writes – but that makes sense. It really does not matter when Oracle reads its data files since it is touching them all the time, so that can be turned off. This is known as setting the noatime file attribute. If this is to be done for just the Oracle data files, the command is chattr +A file_name. If this is to be done to an entire directory, the command is chattr –R +A directory_name. But the best method would be to edit the /etc/fstab and for each entry, add the noatime keyword to the file system parameter list (i.e. the fourth column). This ensures that the entire set of file systems benefit from this technique – and more importantly, that the setting persists across reboots. Below is an example of the necessary fstab file entries.

```
/dev/sda1        /boot        ext3        defaults,noatime    1 1
/dev/sda2        /            ext3        defaults,noatime    1 2
/dev/sda3        /home        ext3        defaults,noatime    1 3
```

The third and final Linux preparatory suggestion is to modify the Linux kernel parameters to best support Oracle by adding the following entries to the /etc/sysctl.conf file.

```
kernel.shmmax = 2147483648
kernel.sem = 250 32000 100 128
fs.file-max = 65536
fs.aio-max-nr = 1048576
net.ipv4.ip_local_port_range = 1024 65000
net.core.rmem_default = 262144
net.core.rmem_max = 262144
net.core.wmem_default = 262144
net.core.wmem_max = 262144
```

# Prepare the Database Configuration

As with operating systems, there are also entire collections of books written on the subject of tuning and optimizing database performance. So again it would be unreasonable to try to cover such a broad and exhaustive topic in this book. But nonetheless there are likewise some major and important database settings to verify setting properly in order to obtain the most indicative results. The following two sections will cover several such settings for SQL Server and Oracle.

## SQL Server

SQL Server is a relatively easy to administrate database platform. Most of its more important configuration settings are self-tuning and self-managing. Things like memory, CPU utilization, and session control are all handled automatically for the benefit of the DBA and support team.

However, there are several system-wide settings within SQL Server that are tempting to adjust but should only be tinkered with once benchmarking has progressed to the utmost extremes of scalability. These configuration parameters can have a disproportionately large impact upon various benchmarking results, usually slowing things down on lower-end benchmarks by causing additional system overhead. Therefore it is quite advantageous to configure all those settings using the following advice.

- Affinity Mask

    - Enables the database professional to selectively specify which CPUs, on a multi-CPU SMP server, will service SQL Server requests. For example, the affinity mask setting can be used to run SQL Server only on CPUs 2 and 4 on a 4-CPU system.

    - Rarely helps, when adjusted from the default, and often makes things worse because Windows must do a lot of additional handling for the manually defined CPU handling.

- Lightweight Pooling

    - Enables sessions to run on individual Windows fibers, rather than on the larger Windows threads.

    - Only useful on large SMP multi-proc machines where all CPUs are maxed or nearly maxed and > 20,000 context switching occur per second.

- Max Worker Threads

    - By default, SQL Server uses a preset number of worker threads according to its own internal formulas (usually 255 max worker threads). This behavior sets aside a pool of threads to service requests to SQL Server and to manage the MemToLeave area of memory.

    - Some people confuse worker threads with users and try to increase this number to be more like the number of users connecting to the database. Do not do this! Do not change this number without very good cause! SQL Server does an exceptional job of pooling worker threads for many users.

- Parallelism
    - Tells SQL Server to split very large queries up into streams that can be run in parallel on multiple CPUs simultaneously.

    - Do not enable parallelism without major testing because the overhead of splitting and merging streams is very heavy. Only a very specific type of query benefits from parallelism, while other types of queries and transactions suffer a degradation of performance. Therefore, it is a very good idea not to tamper with this setting.

- Priority Boost
    - Controls whether services are run as lower priority in the background or higher priority in the foreground.

    - Leave set to 0, especially on clusters, so that SQL Server handles which services get priority. This ensures that the OS never starves for processor priority.

- Set Working Set Size
    - Controls how SQL Server acquires memory. When enabled, SQL Server does not release the dynamic memory it acquires thus "setting" or fixing the memory working set size.

    - Leave set to 0 so that SQL Server can dynamically give and take memory between SQL Server and the OS as needed.

A couple database settings should also be mentioned. SQL Server is, by default, configured to automatically grow databases as needed. This is a very expensive I/O operation and should be avoided on both benchmarking and production systems. Consequently, databases should be created of sufficient size so that they will not have to autogrow during benchmark tests. This is especially true for the tempdb system database which is used to house temporary data structures during the normal operation of the database. We recommend that tempdb is set, when installing SQL Server, to at least 25% of the size of the database that is being benchmarked or 250mb, whichever is more.

## Oracle

Several Oracle configuration parameters can have a disproportionately large impact upon various benchmarking results. Therefore it is quite advantageous to configure all those settings using the following advice.

First and foremost, it is critical to get Oracle to perform asynchronous I/O assuming the disk subsystem will support it. For Oracle versions 10g release 2 and higher – this is compiled in as the default. But prior to that, DBAs had to re-compile and re-link Oracle to guarantee this by doing the following.

- Going to the Oracle Home directory and rebuilding the Oracle binaries:
  - cd $ORACLE_HOME/rdbms/lib
  - make -f ins_rdbms.mk async_on
  - make -f ins_rdbms.mk ioracle
- Setting requisite associated init.ora or spfile asynch parameter settings:
  - disk_asynch_io = true
  - filesystemio_options = setall

Next an appropriate Oracle block size must be chosen. Now popular belief is that larger block sizes translate into lower rates of sustainable concurrency. The theory is that more users accessing data concurrently means more likelihood of users needing to access the same blocks' data and incurring waits or locks. However empirical testing does not support this premise.

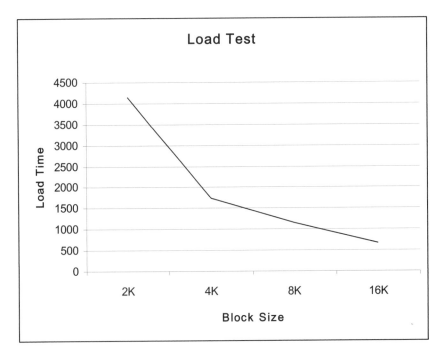

**Figure 5.1:** *Time to load database objects with different block sizes*

Figure 5.1 illustrates that as the Oracle block size increases, the time to load database objects decreases – as one would expect. These results are of course quite understandable. The database engine has less internal block allocation requests to fulfill in order to process the same amount of raw data (since each block can hold more data as its size increases, less blocks are thus necessary). But what about the sustainable transactions per second rates, how do they fare as the block size increases?

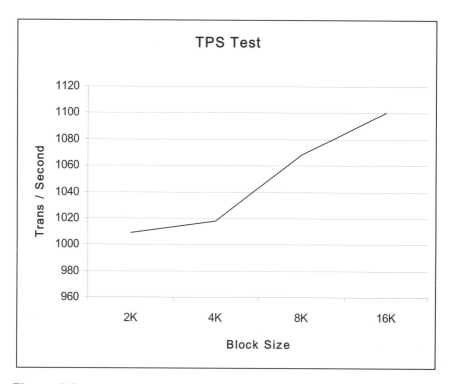

**Figure 5.2:** *Transaction per second rate with different block sizes*

Figure 5.2 clearly demonstrates although quite unexpectedly, that the sustainable transaction per second rate also increases as the block size grows. This seems quite at odds with common sense – at least until one digs a little further. The explanation lies in the scaling factor of the database being tested. As the number of concurrent users increases, the database size typically increases as well. Thus the data access requests are spread across a larger universe, and thus the chance for collisions, waits and competing locks is reduced.

Finally, the database professional must choose Oracle SGA memory allocation values that accommodate the benchmark size and nature, plus considers operating system overheads and limitations. For example, the Oracle SGA size limit on 32-bit operating systems is generally around 1.7 GB. Assuming one has a database server with 4GB of RAM and that a benchmark for a maximum of 2000 concurrent users will be run, what sizes make sense. If we assume that each Oracle server process will require around ½ a megabyte, then the server will need about a gigabyte for all the operating processes that will be spawned. Thus allocation of the entire limit of 1.7 GB SGA probably makes sense. In fact if Oracle offers an extended SGA size for that operating system, then a larger size might even be advisable. Regardless, below are the main parameters that must be considered when calculating Oracle's primary SGA allocation needs.

### Oracle 9i

```
db_block_size
db_cache_size=(SGA_MAX/db_block_size) - shared_pool_size
pga_aggregate_size
shared_pool_size
workarea_size_policy=AUTO
```

### Oracle 10g

```
pga_aggregate_size
sga_target_size=SGA_MAX
workarea_size_policy=AUTO
```

## Concentrate on What and not How

In order to more readily and reliably benchmark database performance, it is advisable to use an industry standard tool – such as Quest Software's Benchmark Factory (BMF). The idea is to make the testing process simple, and thus permit the tester to concentrate on the test results rather than the test process. Benchmark Factory excels in that pursuit. With Benchmark Factory, users can within mere moments select, modify and submit an industry standard benchmark like the TPC-C or TPC-H – and all without knowing anything other than what database to run the test against and for how many concurrent users. Benchmark Factory knows what database objects to build, what data to load for the size database necessary to support that many users, then simply does all the work necessary to score and record the test.

Thus users truly can liberate themselves from the test's internal implementation methodologies and requirements. Now some DBAs may feel this robs them of control. But the truth is that these benchmarks are very complex and highly demanding – with deviations from specification resulting in suspect results. Furthermore, standards organizations controlling benchmarks often charge for access to the implementation details for those tests. So using a tool like Benchmark Factory indemnifies one from such undo risks and unnecessary costs. Benchmarking truly should be about the destination, and not the journey to get there.

## Installing Benchmark Factory

Benchmark Factory is a Microsoft Windows based software solution, with several key component parts. The BMF graphical user interface (a.k.a. the BMF Console) is used to design benchmark tests, manage their execution, and examine the posted results. There is also a MySQL database installed with benchmark Factory that holds all test execution metrics and statistics. Thus experienced users can query that database with external reporting tools in addition to using the Benchmark Factory Console. There is also an optional Benchmark Factory Agent – which is used to execute large numbers of concurrent tests. The agent can also be installed and run simultaneously on several other Windows machines, and they will be detected and used by the main Benchmark Factory Console. Thus the basic overall Benchmark Factory software architecture is that shown in Figure 5.3.

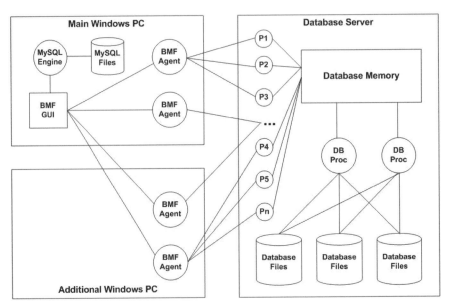

**Figure 5.3:** *Benchmark Factory Architecture*

When setting up Benchmark Factory, users may actually need to perform several installs – the full install on the primary Windows PC used to launch the BMF Console, house the MySQL BMF repository, and manage all the BMF Agents (whether they are on the same or different PCs). Additional installs may then be necessary to place agents on other PCs.

There is really just one main reason for needing agents installed across multiple machines like this – to distribute concurrent user loads across the hardware so as not to overload any one Windows PC. Benchmark Factory will equally distribute its concurrent user load across all automatically detected agents (although you may need to turn off any firewalls or open ports on the BMF Console PC). In fact the BMF Console shows what agents are available and how currently running jobs have been equally allocated as shown in Figure 5.4.

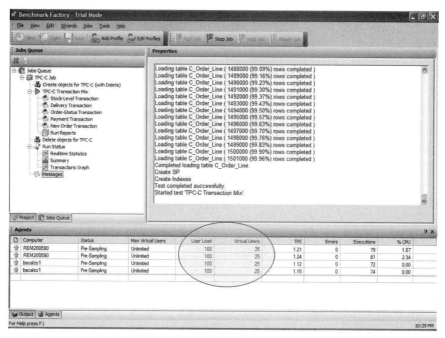

**Figure 5.4:** *Benchmark Factory's console displays running load agents, user load and performance metrics*

When launching the agent on remote Windows PC's, users will need to inform those agents which BMF Console they should be communicating and coordinating with. That process is very simple. From the Main Menu, select Settings -> Options and the screen shown in Figure 5.5 will open. Simply place the desired managing BMF Console machine's IP address or network name. That agent will then coordinate with that BMC Console, as will apply to all agents on that machine going forward (i.e. setting this once will affect all agents launched on that machine).

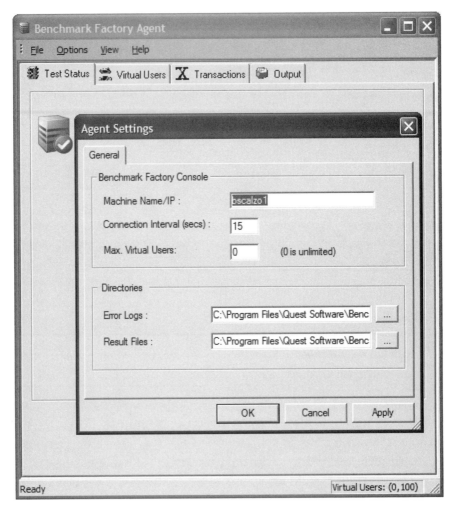

**Figure 5.5:** *Benchmark Factory's Agent Configuration Settings*

# Conclusion

The cumulative process of preparing for effective and efficient database benchmarking is neither entirely obvious nor overly trivial as a whole – although all the individual steps are fairly simple.

This chapter presented information on how to effectively configure low-level operating systems for database benchmarking, whether a Linux or Windows Server. It also shared a great deal of information on how to properly configure database servers for optimal performance.

SQL Server provides a number of parameters for tuning performance. However, SQL Server does an exceptional job of dynamically scheduling and allocating resources. Tampering with the performance parameters of SQL Server is almost always counter-productive except at the very extremes of scalability and under situations where the tuner knows the *exact* interaction of the workload and system overhead.

Oracle, on the other hand, has many more parameters which are configurable and must be set by the DBA to achieve optimal performance. While these settings are not dynamically self-adjusting, they provide the DBA with opportunities to control and maintain the configuration settings themselves.

# Running the
# Benchmarks

*A full redesign?*

*No chance!*

*I'm tired of throwing money at Oracle problems!*

*Just move it to a faster server!*

Chief
Information
Officer

"The buck stops here"

# Selecting among Benchmarks

The necessary first step to effective and useful benchmarking is deciding what specifically it is one wants to test. Now this is a very subjective exercise that can be answered differently by different people, or even differently by the same people at different times. There really is no single, definitive benchmark to run under all circumstances – it all kind of depends. Nonetheless there are some useful guidelines detailed back in chapter 2 about what each benchmark was designed to test. However one should not feel compelled to strictly adhere to the original benchmarking specification or guidelines entirely, as there will obviously be mitigating or special circumstances in many real-world scenarios.

For example, we performed a comprehensive Oracle 10g Real Application Cluster (RAC) scalability test as a joint partnership initiative with a major hardware vendor. Quest Software's Benchmark Factory was used as the standard testing tool of course. In the first study, the standard TPC-C benchmark was used to illustrate how adding RAC nodes to the cluster increased the maximum sustainable concurrent user load in an approximately linear fashion as shown in Figure 6.1.

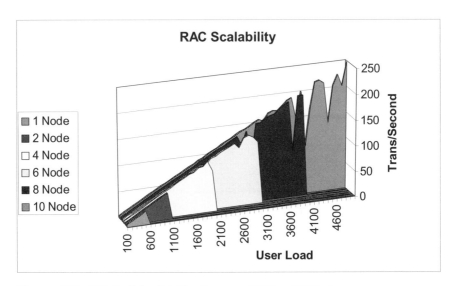

**Figure 6.6:** *TPC-C Scalability for 1 to 10 RAC Nodes.*

The goal of this test was to demonstrate that Oracle's claims about RAC scalability for increased user demands is as simple as just adding more nodes. For this particular hardware vendor, the users per node "sweet spot" was about 600 for a typical dual Xeon based server. We could have very easily used other benchmarks for this test, but decided that the standard TPP-C benchmark was a good general purpose test for illustrating typical application demands for this type of scenario. The complete study can be viewed at:

www.bertscalzo.com/uploads/ORACLE_10G_RAC_SCALABI LITY_LESSONS_LEARNED.pdf

For the second study, we tested the scalability of the new Intel Xeon multi-core processors versus their single-core ancestors. But first, a little history to put this second study in perspective is in order.

> The steps involved in running a benchmark against Microsoft SQL Server are essentially the same as running a benchmark against Oracle. However, we will show any major differences as we go along.

Multi-core processors are a hot commodity right now and are all the rage both in the press and peoples' more recent new server configuration planning. The chief problem that multi-core CPUs directly address is the numerous technical challenges related to heat generation and dissipation with ever increasing clock speeds. As Intel's Xeon chip designers ran into the "brick wall" or upper limits on reasonable clock speeds and heat management, exciting new technologies evolved to fulfill the need for more raw processing power without increased heat. The resulting new technologies have thrust us on a clear and steady path toward the world of parallel computing.

Back in 2002, Intel introduced "Hyperthreading", which enabled CPUs to sometimes process multiple threads in parallel using just a single core via highly efficient instruction scheduling, resource allocation, and instruction execution. While not genuinely a multi-core processor, hyperthreading was nonetheless an extremely important and significant first step toward parallel processing. It clearly proved that raw processing power could be increased without requiring faster clock speeds. It was like finding a higher gear on your automobile.

And while published results ranged from 20% to 40% overall improvement, the consensus was that circumstances had to be just right and software had to be written to take full advantage of it. Because when conditions were not correct, the CPU pipeline would stall and occasionally deliver slightly worse performance.

But now Intel offers 100% genuine dual-core processors in which each chip offers two full cores. It is much like putting two four cylinder engines under the hood of one car. Moreover, hyperthreading has been retained thus offering automobiles with both dual engines and higher gears. And if those improvements were not enough, the new multi-core CPUs also offer better heat characteristics than their single core brethren. Thus multi-core processors offer numerous advantages, including:

- Increased performance per server rack slot.

- Decreased direct power consumption for CPUs.

- Decreased indirect power consumption for cooling.

- Relatively inexpensive and very easy upgrade paths.

But just how much "bang for the buck" can database professionals realistically obtain while using the new multi-core processors? The common misperception is approximately twice the raw processing power – or very near to it. But could two four cylinder engines simply glued together ever really challenge a big-block V8? We think not! But fortunately, Intel is publishing a very realistic and believable figure of 53% average overall performance gain. It is refreshing to see such reasonable rough estimates from a hardware vendor.

The purpose of the second study was to verify that the observed percentage improvements hold true for real-world type usage. Thus we tested a four node Oracle 10g RAC cluster using Benchmark Factory's CPU performance scalability test (a subset of the scalability benchmark focusing on just CPU which made sense given the relative CPU comparative nature of this study).

First the benchmark was run using single core Xeon CPUs, and then again on the exact same hardware after swapping in the new dual core Xeon CPUs (i.e. same clock speed, cache, etc.). The overall test results were in-line with our expectations – the new dual-core processors utilized in an Oracle 10g RAC environment yielded quite explainable and predictable scalability as shown in Figure 6.2.

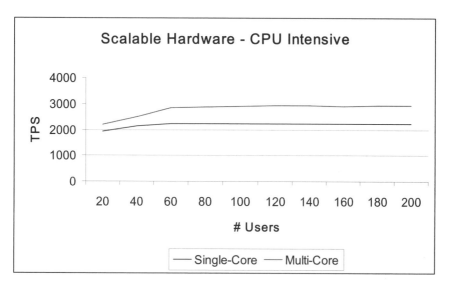

**Figure 6.7:** *Single vs. Dual Core Scalable Hardware Test.*

A later section of this chapter further examines the typical factors monitored during such testing, and the next chapter shows how to extrapolate such data into meaningful results (which in this case just happen to almost perfectly match Intel's 53% overall improvement claims even though Figure 6.2's numbers may not make that readily apparent). So read on.

# Creating Benchmark Jobs

Using a tool like Benchmark Factory, the task of creating and customizing a benchmark is a snap. Most users (with little or no knowledge of the various TPC or other industry standard benchmarks) will find themselves defining and executing benchmark jobs in a mere matter of minutes. Here is a brief synopsis of the benchmark project creation process which is entirely wizard driven.

First launch the Benchmark Factory Console (i.e. GUI) and simply choose Main Menu->File->New, which will open the New Project creation dialog. Next choose to create the new project as a standard benchmark, followed by choosing from a list of industry standard benchmarks with their descriptions. Now a profile selection screen displays. You can either choose pre-existing profile from the drop-down list or press the "New" button to create one.

A profile is nothing more than a named database connection; simply record a name, a database user-id and password, and possibly a default database or tablespace depending on the database you are working with. Some of these profiles (such as Oracle and SQL Server) can opt for native connections, which are generally better performing than other connection methods.

But profiles may use ODBC connections as well, but this requires the additional step of opening the Windows ODBC wizard and defining the necessary ODBC connection info (plus having the appropriate ODBC drivers installed, of course). After completing the above steps, the screen in Figure 6.3 will appear.

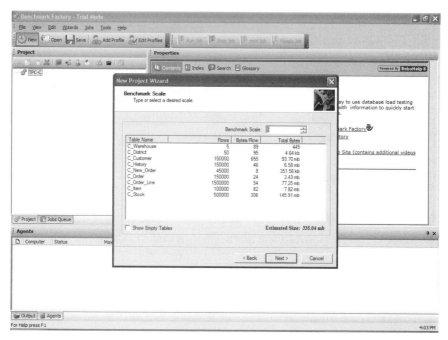

**Figure 6.8:** *New Project Wizard's Database Scaling Factor.*

You now need to define the size of the database that Benchmark Factory will create and populate to run the benchmark against. It knows all the right tables and indexes to create, but it does need the user to define the relative size of the database to use. This is known as choosing the benchmark scale factor. Note that the bigger the scale factor, obviously the longer it will take to create and load those objects.

For most tests, the scale factor should equal the test's maximum concurrent user load. So if you are going to run a Scalability benchmark with 1000 users, a scale factor of 1000 should also be chosen. There is however one notable exception to this rule – the TPP-C benchmark. In the case of TPC-C, the specification mandates that 10 concurrent users can run per warehouse. Therefore for the TPC-C, the maximum number of concurrent users is divided by ten to arrive at the proper scale factor. So for 1000 users, you would choose a scale of 100 (i.e. 1000 / 10).

Finally, you need to define the number of test iterations and the number of concurrent users per iteration to benchmark. Figure 6.4 shows that there will be ten test iterations, starting with 100 up to 1000 users, and in increments of 100. Users can choose whatever starting, ending and intervals they like, but should realize that test iterations consume time to execute. For example a TPC-C test often takes about four minutes per iteration to run (plus a little overhead). So using the values chosen in Figure 6.4, the overall benchmark will run for approximately 40 minutes just to process all the intervals.

Furthermore, database creation and load time should not be forgotten. For instance, looking back at Figure 6.3, it shows that we have asked for a 335 megabyte database, which might take another 40 minutes for a total of an hour and twenty minutes to run this one benchmark. But it only took us maybe two minutes to set it up, so just kick it off and go do something else.

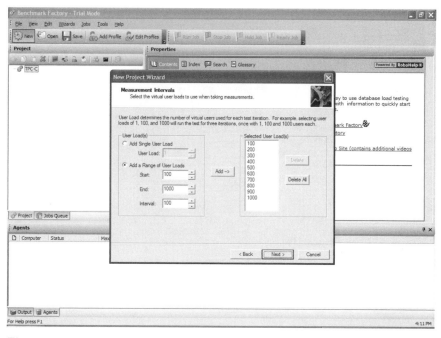

**Figure 6.9:** *New Project Wizard's User Load Scenarios.*

While navigating the benchmark project creation wizard, do not agonize over every decision. Because once a project is completed, it will show up in the tree-view as shown in the left hand side of the screen, Figure 6.5. And from here you can navigate the various nodes on the left hand side, and you will see tabs of different options displayed on the right hand side – all of which can be modified. Thus if you wanted to change my user load of 100 to 1000 by increments of 200, you would just make the change as shown in the right hand side of Figure 6.5.

There are numerous benchmark properties that can be changed including transaction mix ratios and weights. But the more properties you change the further out of spec your test will be and thus the less generally accurate for relative external comparisons. But Benchmark Factory will function with most selections made, so feel free to experiment and create your own specialized versions of tests. Who knows, your customizations may be much more meaningful for your desired purposes and expectations.

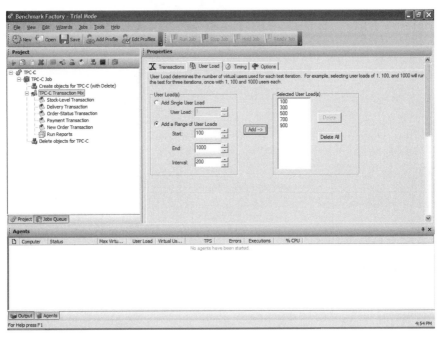

**Figure 6.10:** *Benchmark Factory Project Properties.*

## Running Benchmark Jobs

The process to execute a benchmark project is actually quite simple, just do a right hand mouse menu click over the project and choose "Submit Job". If your profile information for establishing the database connection is accurate, the Benchmark Factory will initiate, monitor and score the test. Not too much that can go wrong actually. The software assumes that it should execute the entire benchmark the same way every time – that is to create the database objects, load them and then run the SQL commands which comprise the benchmark.

But rarely do users perform isolated one time runs. Often, users want to run a sub-test (i.e. a subset of the test), see the results and then run another test against the same sized database. This is often referred to as iterative benchmarking. For example you might create a scale of 1000, but first run a sample test iteration of just 100 users to verify that the benchmark works as planned. That way any obvious and minor issues can be fixed or tuned. Then the test would be repeated for larger and larger iterations, until the maximum scale factor is reached.

But using the benchmark we constructed in Figure 6.5, we would have to incur the cost of rebuilding the 335 megabyte database for each run. Because if you examine the tree-view back in Figure 6.5, you will see that the steps are: create and load the data, run the mixed workload and then drop the database objects. Imagine if you are doing a large data warehousing test (e. g. TPC-H) with a 10 terabyte sized database. Even on very fast hardware, it could take a whole day for just one run to create and load that size of data. So you would be doing 98% data loads and 2% benchmark runs, which is not very efficient.

The solution is actually quite easy to implement. Look at Figure 6.6 below. We have simply created two benchmark projects. The first one creates the database objects and loads them. The second one just runs the benchmark's workload. So returning to our 10 terabyte data warehousing example, we would run the first project and then have the DBA do either an export or backup. That way we can simply do restores of those massive amounts of data more quickly and without relying on Benchmark Factory. Then we can perform iterative benchmarking by simply repetitively running the second project after each external restore.

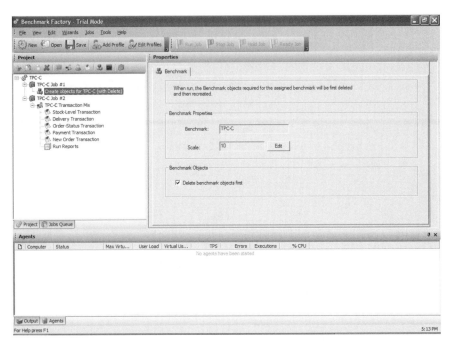

**Figure 6.11:** *Benchmark Factory Database Creation Project.*

Of course that makes the overall restore and execute process more manual, which means more work and more chance of mistakes. But not to worry, Benchmark Factory has the ability to call external scripts. So for those whose database is local to their benchmark Factory Console machine, the restore command may be able to be added to the benchmark's workload using the options tab as shown in Figure 6.7. In fact, it is probably even possible to do so for remote databases as well – assuming the script can properly initiate the load from the Benchmark Factory Console machine. We have seen clever people use Windows batch scripts to ftp files over to a UNIX server and then re-execute a database load command. The only limits are the user's imagination and scripting abilities.

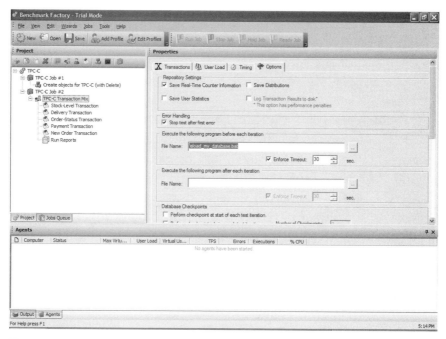

**Figure 6.12:** *Project Property for calling External Program.*

# Monitoring Benchmark Runs

Let's return now to the second study and see how to monitor the benchmark's execution behavior – looking for potential bottlenecks or trouble spots. We need to monitor the database, operating system, network and I/O subsystem (i.e. Oracle's Automatic Storage Management) all at once for potential problems. And while a specific tool, Quest's Spotlight on RAC, will be used here to keep that process simple and thus permit us to focus again on the what and not the how, there are numerous less user friendly ways to collect the same information. But Spotlight on RAC (and Spotlight on SQL Server, for Microsoft SQL Server database platform) permits users to easily show via simple screen snapshots numerous potential and interesting internal performance issues without overwhelming readers.

For example, we could have used the Linux commands such as vmstat, iostat and sar, plus tools like Oracle's Enterprise Manager to watch most of the same metrics. But there are two major drawbacks to such an approach with both Oracle and SQL Server. First, we would have had to use multiple unrelated tools and correlate disparate but potentially correlated results across those tools – something that is easier said than done. And second, we would have to know about typical versus problematic values and reliably spot them among large amounts of raw collected data.

Whereas the Spotlight tools (on Oracle RAC and on Microsoft SQL Server) are designed to provide a comprehensive, yet very comprehendible overview of numerous database internals visualized by a world-class dash-board like display that makes clustered database monitoring and diagnostics a snap. With its simple street-light like color coded scheme (where green is good and red is bad), plus its point-and-click to drill-down into details design – DBAs can easily monitor their clusters in order to detect, diagnose and correct all potential problems and hotspots. Spotlight on RAC, shown in Figure 6.8, and Spotlight on SQL Server, shown in Figure 6.9, even offers alarms with automatic prioritization and weighted rankings to help less experienced DBAs focus their attention on more critical or problematic issues.

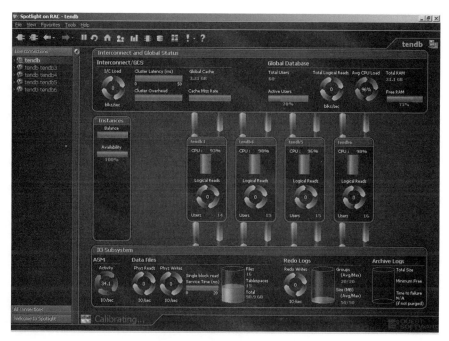

**Figure 6.8:** *Spotlight on Oracle RAC.*

Similarly, we could use Windows Performance Monitor and SQL Profiler on Microsoft SQL Server to fully track and then correlate the performance load on Microsoft SQL Server. Doing so takes a lot of time and energy, so Spotlight on SQL Server enables us to make the most of our time. Figure 6.9 shows Spotlight on SQL Server while monitoring a database server under load.

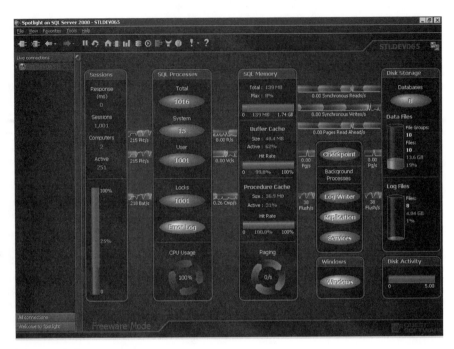

**Figure 6.9:** *Spotlight on SQL Server.*

Returning to our second study, we monitored both scenarios (single core versus multi core) when the test load hit 60 concurrent users. Looking back at Figure 6.8, Spotlight on RAC shows that each server node was averaging around 96% CPU utilization. (Identical information on SQL Server's resource consumption is available in Spotlight on SQL Server.)

Furthermore, when we drilled down into a particular node's operating system level information, the results clearly showed that the "Load Average/Run Queue" rapidly had ramped up to over 16 processes deep with a significantly increasing slope as shown in Figure 6.10. And deep run queues are the harbinger of processor overloading. Clearly all four RAC server nodes were very highly stressed. And even though sufficient memory was available to prevent swapping, the CPU saturation alone was pushing these servers nearly to their limits.

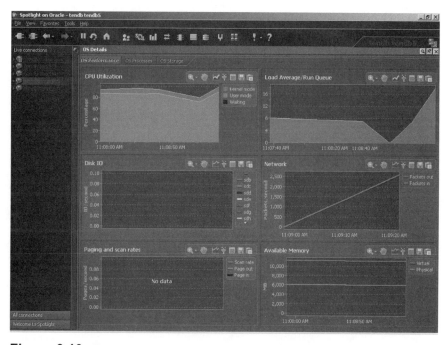

**Figure 6.10:** *Increasing Run Queue Signals CPU Saturation.*

So what happened when we repeated the CPU Intensive Scalable Hardware benchmark with the new multi-core processors? Again, according to Intel literature we should have expected about a 53% improvement. Remember – instead of two physical CPUs each with hyperthreading per node for a total of 4 logical CPUs, we instead now had four physical CPUs each with hyperthreading per node for a total of 8 logical CPUs. In fact doing a LINUX "top" command bore that out – LINUX now saw 8 processors per node.

So now look at Figure 6.11, where under the same 60 concurrent user load, the servers are only an average of 78% utilized. That means each node has about an extra 18% raw processing capacity being under-utilized versus the prior single-core runs. As you can see in the differences between Figures 6.9 and 6.11, Spotlight made this improvement extremely easy to see by the fact that the coloration went from predominantly orange to mostly yellow for the five CPU related graphic displays.

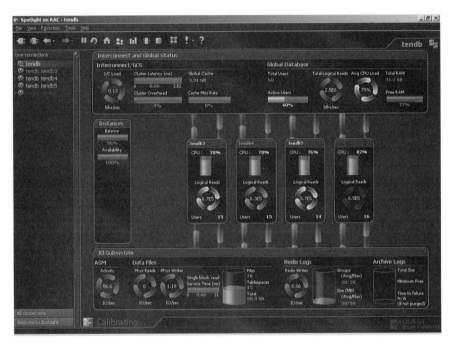

**Figure 6.11:** *Dual Cores CPU's 18% Less Stressed.*

Furthermore the "Load Average/Run Queue" remained between six and eight processes deep or about half as full as before, as shown in Figure 6.12. Moreover, the slope of the line was relatively flat as a whole (i.e. seemed to reach a plateau and level off) as compared to Figure 6.10's obviously increasing and out of control line. This is critical, because a key factor in evaluating processor performance is the average length of the run queue. For as the run queue length increases the perceived performance decreases because of slower response times and longer run times.

The dual-core CPUs obviously handled the load much better than their single-core ancestors – which is as expected. But now we have a qualitative measurement of that improvement for later analysis.

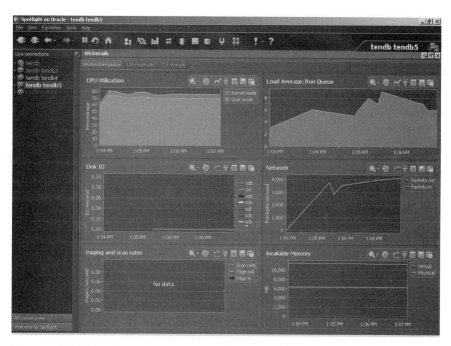

**Figure 12:** *Dual Core CPU's less Run Queue Saturation.*

## Special Oracle RAC Considerations

Finally there are several Oracle Real Application Cluster issues to consider while running benchmark tests. Even though the RAC architecture means that the database is comprised of a group of related physical database servers cooperating as essentially one larger logical database, nonetheless you need to guarantee that the benchmark tests spread their load nearly equally across all the nodes in order to obtain meaningful and reliable results. For those using Oracle 10g Release 2, it is probably best to use Oracle SQL*Net's native load balancing. All that you need to do is to define your Benchmark Factory profile to reference your database SID, and let Oracle balance the load. However for those on earlier versions of Oracle or who simply wish to manager that at the application level, Benchmark Factory provides profile clustering control via a simple properties screen as shown in Figure 6.13. By simply checking "Enable Clustering" and specifying the number of node, Benchmark Factory will automatically submit equal portions of the load to profile's SID with a suffix for each node number. However this requires that the SQL*Net "tnsnames.ora" file has individual entries for each so named cluster SID.

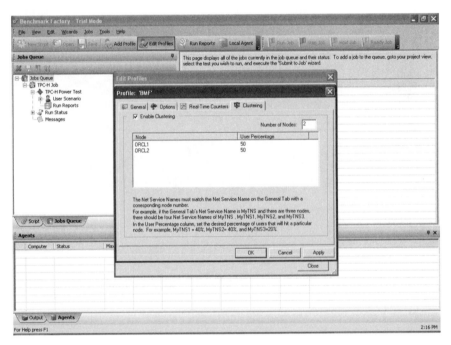

**Figure 6.13:** *Benchmark Factory Profile Settings for Oracle RAC.*

Furthermore, some benchmark tests by their very nature may require fewer concurrent users than nodes (e.g. TPC-H stream test generally max's out at 50 concurrent users). For such tests, the DBA should enable parallel DML to utilize both the multiple processors per node and the multiple nodes per cluster. Thus DDL like the following is often required:

```
ALTER TABLE H_SUPPLIER PARALLEL (DEGREE 8 INSTANCES 4);
ALTER TABLE H_PART     PARALLEL (DEGREE 8 INSTANCES 4);
ALTER TABLE H_PARTSUPP PARALLEL (DEGREE 8 INSTANCES 4);
ALTER TABLE H_CUSTOMER PARALLEL (DEGREE 8 INSTANCES 4);
ALTER TABLE H_ORDER    PARALLEL (DEGREE 8 INSTANCES 4);
ALTER TABLE H_LINEITEM PARALLEL (DEGREE 8 INSTANCES 4);

ALTER INDEX H_partsupp_idx1 PARALLEL (DEGREE 8 INSTANCES 4);
ALTER INDEX H_customer_idx1 PARALLEL (DEGREE 8 INSTANCES 4);
ALTER INDEX H_order_idx1    PARALLEL (DEGREE 8 INSTANCES 4);
ALTER INDEX H_lineitem_idx1 PARALLEL (DEGREE 8 INSTANCES 4);
```

There are yet other questions or issues that need asked when doing benchmarks in a RAC environment, such as:

- How many concurrent users can each node support?

- How many concurrent users can the cluster support?

- Does adding each successive node yield the same gains?

- What's the optimal hardware configuration for each node?

Basically – how scalable is RAC and thus what hardware is needed for a particular project. But that is exactly the type of question one runs benchmarks to answer. Because no matter how much we would like, there really can be no definitive single answer for the question "what hardware do we need". While hardware vendors work very hard to publish standard benchmark results for various platforms, there are simply too many variables for one to easily interpolate those results for their special needs. Hence that is why it is often best to benchmark yourself in order to become more familiar with the performance characteristics of the hardware being used – and thus to have a more reasonable idea of how far you can push the performance envelope. Thinks back to the original "Star Trek" series – Scotty could never have coaxed the engines beyond their specs had he not known them so intimately.

# Conclusion

In this chapter, we walked through the entire process needed to run one or more benchmark tests on Oracle or SQL Server. Examples were presented using the Quest Software's Benchmark Factory tool for creating and running a full benchmarking test, as well as Quest Software's Spotlight tool for correlating performance bottlenecks within the benchmark tests to specific faults within the database platform, such as memory, CPU, or disk I/O.

In the next chapter we will discuss the various means of analyzing and interpreting the results of the benchmark tests and how to use that analysis to your maximum advantage.

# Interpreting Benchmark Results

*I'm predictng that you have trouble ahead.*

*You'se need to consider our affordable insurance.*

# Don't Rush to Conclusions

Remember the concept of iterative testing discussed in the previous chapter? Another key reason the iterative testing methodology is so useful is that it is not unusual to have background noise or unexpected skews in your initial benchmark runs – because it is difficult to get all your ducks lined up in a row right from the start. Often a minor misstep in either preparation or configuration will yield results that are off track. In fact, it is not uncommon that such miscalculations can make even the staunchest benchmarking gurus second guess their projects.

# An Example on Oracle

In the first study in chapter 6 we verified Oracle's claims about RAC being highly scalable, though, we ran into a few bumps along the way – bumps which required numerous additional test iterations to correct before we could obtain meaningful benchmark results. Let's walk through that process to see how such issues evolve and hopefully resolve.

A key aspect of this first study was to accurately estimate the maximum number of concurrent users a single node could support (referred to as the "sweet spot") and then double that number for each node added to the cluster. If Oracle's scalability claims were accurate, we should expect a near linear Benchmark Factory transaction/second graph no matter how many nodes were added. Here are the steps we performed:

- Ran TPC-C benchmark for 100 to 800 users with the user load increasing in increments of 100 in order to determine the maximum number of concurrent users a node could reasonably support – a measurement referred to as the "sweet spot".

- Monitored the benchmark execution via the vmstat command, looking for the points at which excessive paging and swapping begins and CPU idle time consistently approaching zero.

- Examined the resulting Benchmark Factory transactions/second graph, looking for a degradation point initiating a clear decline and recorded that point as the "sweet spot".

- Reduced the "sweet spot" number by some reasonable percentage to account for the RAC architecture's and inter- and intra-node overheads (for example, reduce it by 10 percent).

Unfortunately when we ran the benchmark beyond four nodes in the cluster, the scalability dropped off precipitously. Something was wrong with either our assumptions or our test – and very wrong at that! Even though our process looked sound, we made two fundamental mistakes.

First, we should have relied predominately on the operating system metrics (i.e. vmstat) for identifying the performance degradation point. Because even though the Benchmark Factory transactions/second graph continued to increase up to 700 users before tapering off, the vmstat data clearly showed that performance problems started well before that.

Second, our user load increment size was too big. Testing from 100 to 800 users in increments of 100 was not granular enough. So we cut the increment size to 50, that of course meant more iterations than before, with hope that those additional iterations would more clearly show where the performance degradation occurred. Thus through better initial testing, we in fact found the "sweet spot" to be 500 users. Now our benchmarking could continue and thus easily showed that RAC was scalable well beyond just four nodes and many thousands of concurrent users as shown in Figure 7.1.

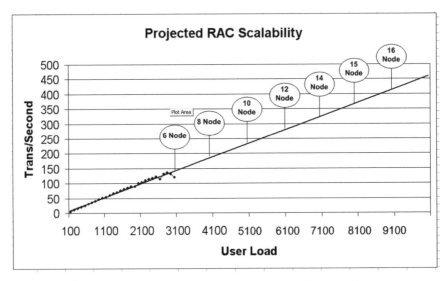

**Figure 7.13:** *Projected RAC Scalability across Multiple CPUs.*

Later when we performed the second study to measure the improvement by switching to dual-core processors, we of course had to first ascertain the new "sweet spot". By again focusing on the operating system metrics (provided by vmstat) to find the performance degradation point, we learned that we also needed to double the server's memory because 1000 users per machine exceeded the capabilities of 4 gigabytes of RAM.

In fact, memory was constrained once the test approached 700 users. So dual-core processors handling twice the load required twice the memory – makes sense when you think about it. We would thus expect quad-core processors to require twice again the memory and next to possibly exceed either the network or I/O bandwidths. So we are also planning to double our network cards, switch to TCP/IP's jumbo-frames – but we expect our EMC SAN to handle the extra load.

# An Example on Microsoft SQL Server

In this example, we needed to test a Microsoft SQL Server database and scale the application and number of transactions as high as possible. The server ran on Windows 2000 Enterprise Server with Service Pack 4 installed and all necessary device drivers. The server was also outfitted with either SQL Server 2000 Enterprise Edition or SQL Server 2005 Enterprise Edition, according to the specific test being performed.

We then created the initial SQL Server database of 1 GB for data and 250 MB for the transaction log and adjusted the size of tempdb to 250mb. The server-wide settings for SQL Server were left at default for both SQL Server 2000 and SQL 2005.

A primary goal of the test was to exhaust the resources available to the database by consuming as much server memory as possible within the limits of the Windows 32-bit OS (about 1.7 GB), disk I/O, CPU, etc. Because the servers had only 4 GB of RAM each, allocating half of the memory to SQL Server itself was sufficient—the remaining memory was shared by the OS and the thousands of dedicated SQL Server processes that Benchmark Factory created as its user load.

## Finding the "Sweet Spot"

As described in the previous section detailing the Oracle example, our next step was to ascertain the reasonable load that each SQL Server instance could accommodate.

This was arguably the most critical aspect of the entire benchmark testing process. We initially ran the benchmark on the SQL Server instance without monitoring the test via Spotlight on SQL Server. Thus, simply looking at the transactions-per-second graph in the Benchmark Factory GUI yielded a deceiving conclusion that the "sweet spot" was approximately 1,500 users on a single instance of SQL Server. Although the transactions per second continued to increase up to 1,750 users on SQL Server 2000, the OS was overstressed and exhibited some disk thrashing characteristics at about 1,000 users. Locking also began to be a problem at 1,000 users on SQL Server 2000. Moreover, we did not temper that value by reducing for system overhead and internal processes, such as checkpointing.

The first attempt at running a series of benchmarks for the SQL Server 2000 instance did not scale reliably or predictably beyond 1,500 users. However, additional benchmarks, run under the watchful eye of Spotlight on SQL Server, revealed excessive paging, swapping or a consistent CPU idle time near zero, as the user load increased to 750 rather than the initially assumed 1,000 concurrent users.

In contrast, SQL Server 2005 was able to scale to 1,000 concurrent users (and beyond) without showing similar levels of resource consumption. In fact, SQL Server 2005 never really hit a resource consumption wall (unlike SQL Server 2000). Conversely, Figure 7.2 reveals that across all transactions, SQL Server 2005 (lower line) consistently outperformed SQL Server 2000 (upper line) at all levels of user load.

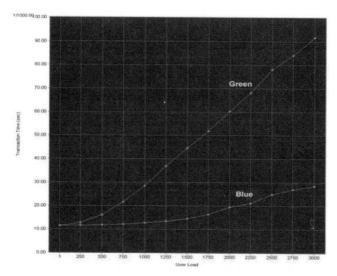

**Figure 7.2:** *Comparison of average transaction times under load generated by Benchmark Factory.*

As shown in Figure 7.2, SQL Server 2000 required longer periods of time to complete a transaction as the user load increased. In other words, as the user load grew, the average transaction time on SQL Server 2000 grew geometrically. SQL Server 2005, with its superior caching algorithms, maintained better throughput at all user loads. Although SQL Server 2005 was not immune to lengthening transaction times as the user load grew from 1,000 concurrent users to 3,000 concurrent users, overall transaction times were much shorter. Even at the peak of 3,000 concurrent users, SQL Server 2005 completed transactions in a fraction of the time required on SQL Server 2000.

During the entire testing process, performance was monitored using Spotlight on SQL Server to identify any problems. As shown in Figure 7.3, SQL Server 2000 had locking difficulties as it scaled the user load. When user loads reached around 500 users, Spotlight on SQL Server revealed that locking was becoming a potential bottleneck and that CPU consumption was becoming critical. By the time the user load reached 1,000 concurrent users, CPU was completely maxed out.

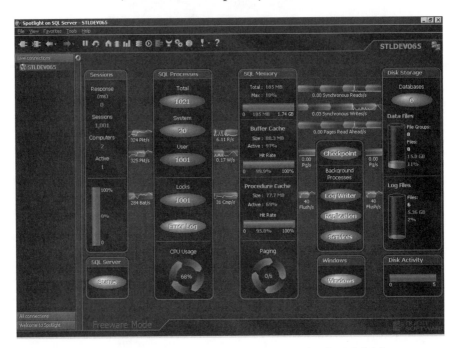

**Figure 7.3:** *Spotlight on SQL Server 2005 at a load of 1,000 concurrent users.*

Figure 7.3 shows, that while SQL Server 2005 was not having an altogether easy time, it was also only using 68 percent of total CPU resources.

Figure 7.4 shows the final Benchmark Factory results for each SQL Server instance and the user load scenarios tested. These results show that both SQL Server 2000 (lower line) and SQL Server 2005 (upper line) scaled predictably as users were added. The scalability was near linear because of transaction caching. However, SQL Server 2005 began to show the strength of its superior query optimizer and memory management as it scaled higher than the 500 user mark. At the 500 concurrent user mark,

SQL Server 2000 began to fall behind, while SQL Server 2005 continued scaling without any issues well beyond 1,500 concurrent users.

We also monitored the storage subsystem using Spotlight on SQL Server. As shown in Figure 7.4, the Spotlight on SQL Server performance graphs indicated that SQL Server 2005 performed well at the peak of SQL Server 2000's scalability testing as considerable capacity was still available to the newer version of SQL Server.

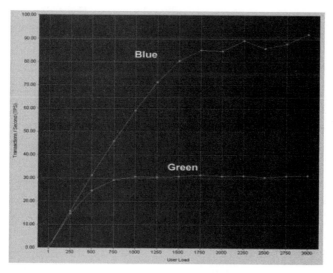

**Figure 7.4:** *Peak and projected performance for SQL Server 2005 (upper line) and SQL Server 2000 (lower line).*

SQL Server 2005 achieved extremely fast service times, with performance reaching more than 2,500 I/Os per second. As the Spotlight on SQL Server results show, SQL Server 2005 performance was predictable and reliable when the test added more users.

# When Conclusions are not Self-Evident

In our previous two examples, we were presented with very straightforward testing requirements that were rather easy to decipher. In our test cases for both the Oracle and Microsoft SQL Server scenarios, we simply wanted to compare the performance of two alternate configurations.

Admittedly, we made the testing much easier on ourselves by changing only one significant component between each test. For the Oracle test, we added an additional node to the Oracle RAC environment each time we scaled our stress test higher. For the Microsoft SQL Server test, we alternated between SQL Server 2000 and SQL Server 2005. All other aspects of the test remained unchanged.

Often a DBA is attempting to tune or optimize a server and can use a standard benchmark as the driver in reaching that goal. In a situation like this, the test is essentially unchanged between each run. It remains "equal" in all scenarios. The single major change monitored by the benchmark test is the *key differentiator*.

Remember: Never alter more than one attribute of the database platform between tests. Otherwise, it will be very difficult, if not impossible, to determine which change on the database platform resulted in any measurable difference in the benchmark results.

When the initial reports produced during benchmarking tests are insufficient for clearly determining an outcome to the test, you must dig deeper into the behavior of the OS and underlying systems. For example, in the earlier Microsoft SQL Server, we used the simple measurement of transactions per second. However, when transactions per second were inconclusive, we drilled deeper into memory and disk queue lengths. These OS level metrics told us that, although the relative number of transactions between two of the tests might have been the same, SQL Server 2005 was outperforming SQL Server 2000 because of short queues for memory and disk.

## Correlating Results

As we mentioned in the previous section, when high-level metrics are not enough to make an accurate determination we need to correlate the performance metrics of lower-level OS subsystems with the behavior of the database.

For example, returning once again to the second study from chapter 6 where we wanted to quantify the improvements by switching to dual-core processors, the graph in Figure 7.5 resulted.

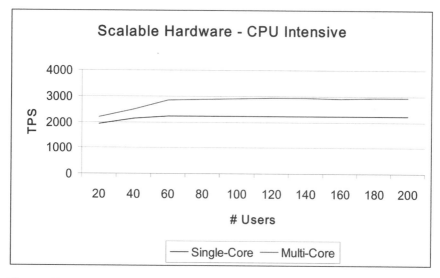

**Figure 7.5:** *Oracle RAC CPU scalability.*

We can deduce two interesting points from Figure 7.5. First, that the benefit of a multi-core processor cannot be truly measured until a sufficient load develops to differentiate between the two CPU architectures. That is why the multi-core CPU line increases between zero and sixty users before leveling off.

Second, the difference between these TPS lines stops at around 32% increased processing power for the multi-core CPU. But why did we not see 53% improvement as advertised?

Remember in chapter 6 we noticed that there was about 18% extra CPU capacity still to spare. So 32% plus 18% yields 50%. That is pretty darn close to the expected results of Intel's advertised 53%. Plus remember, the run queue was half as full too. So it is possible that the results are skewed a bit by other factors, such as RAC inter-node communication and other RAC overheads. But a relatively simple and cheap upgrade that yields approximately a 50% overall improvement without the system becoming as taxed is a clear success.

## Real-time versus "Run" Reports

Typically, when you run a test, you will want to assess results both in real-time as the tests are run and in a saved format to review the results after the fact. Benchmark Factory provides testing results that are easy to interpret and allows you to attribute individual results to individual tasks and users. You can easily monitor high-level database metrics (e.g. transactions/sec), and you can also correlate these benchmarks against low-level OS values such as CPU or memory consumption.

Figure 7.6 gives an example of the real-time performance metrics that can be captured using Benchmark Factory. In most cases the graphs are presented in the most meaningful form. Benchmark

Factory's graphing tool allows you to customize graphs to tailor your load testing viewing requirements.

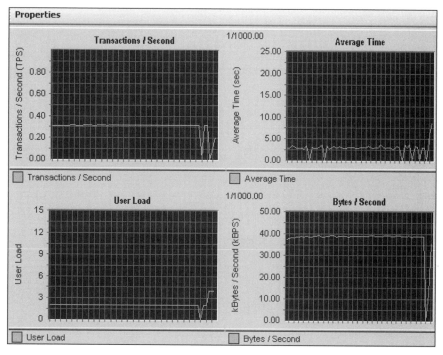

**Figure 7.6:** *Real-time Performance Metrics.*

Benchmark Factory provides the following high-level, real-time testing results:

- Average Response Time
- Average Time
- Bytes/Second
- Deadlocks
- Errors
- Maximum Response Time
- Maximum Time

- Minimum Response Time
- Minimum Time
- Rows/Second
- Total Bytes
- Total Rows
- Transactions/Second
- User Load

Benchmark Factory can also be used to pull summaries of important metrics in real-time, as shown in Figure 7.7.

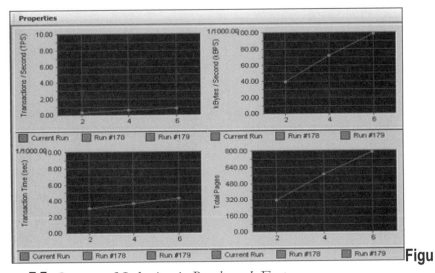

**Figure 7.7:** *Summary Node view in Benchmark Factory.*

The Real Time Statistics provides the following benchmark results:

- Bytes/Second
- Rows/Second

- Total Bytes

- Total Errors

- Total Rows

- Transaction Times

- Transactions/Second

In addition to the real-time metrics, you can track while the benchmark runs, and you have the opportunity to run more sophisticated reports in Benchmark Factory's run mode. For example, Benchmark Factory has a facility to run reports off of all benchmark runs, as shown in Figure 7.8.

**Run Reports**
Select the run(s) to view, compare, or delete.

Show runs that meet the following criteria
Profile: All Profiles          Status: All Runs

| Run | Comment | Status | Profile | Driver | Start Time | End Time |
|-----|---------|--------|---------|--------|-----------|----------|
| 8 | AS3AP Job 20, 40, 60, 80 User Load | Completed | SQL | Microsoft SQL Server (Native) | 02/17/06 13:21:49 | 02/17/06 13:26:16 |
| 5 | AS3AP Job 80, 100, 120, 140 User Load | Completed | SQL | Microsoft SQL Server (Native) | 02/13/06 13:58:38 | 02/13/06 14:14:47 |

**Figure 7.8:** *Run Reports in Benchmark Factory.*

Whether you are viewing a real-time or historical graph, Benchmark Factory uses the same graphing tool. In most cases the graphs are presented in a meaningful and immediately useful form. This graphing tool also allows you to create customized graphs to tailor your load testing viewing requirements.

At a top level, Benchmark Factory produces a nice run report that describes all of the parameters of the benchmarking test as shown in Figure 7.9.

| Run Information | | | |
|---|---|---|---|
| **Test Run Id** | 3 | **Status** | Completed |
| **Start Time** | 02/07/05 14:13:49 | **Stop Time** | 02/07/05 14:21:48 |
| **Comment** | | | |
| 1, 20, 40, 60, 80 User Load | | | |

| Profile Information | |
|---|---|
| **Profile Name** | Oracle |
| **Driver Name** | Oracle |
| **Net Service Name** | test92.prod.quest.corp |
| **Tablespace** | test |
| **User Name** | system |
| **Password** | ****** |

**Maximum Server Throughput**

| User Load | TPS | kBPS | Avg. Response Time | Avg. Transaction Time | Total Executions | Total Rows | Total Errors |
|---|---|---|---|---|---|---|---|
| 80 | 638.75 | 30.009 | 0.069 | 0.000 | 28729 | 28717 | 0 |

**Figure 7.9:** *Run Report.*

There are many more options available for run reports from Benchmark Factory, as illustrated by the wide variety of graphics in this and other chapters. It also allows you to easily do comparison graphics, such as that shown earlier in Figure 7.4.

# Extrapolation & Interpolation

*Extrapolation*, according to Wikipedia, is the process of constructing new data points outside a discrete set of known data points; while *interpolation* is a method of constructing new data points from within a discrete set of known data points. Extrapolation and interpolation are often accompanied by *curve fitting*, in which a function is used to deduce the new data points we might be trying to construct. Curve fitting is the means by which we can inject extrapolated or interpolated values on a pretty graph for our benchmark report.

These two techniques can be very useful in fleshing out testing results in situations where there are related values, but not the exact value we wish to report on.

Here is a very simple example of interpolation. We have a set of values:

| User Load | Trans/Sec |
|-----------|-----------|
| 10 | 400 |
| 20 | 500 |
| 40 | 100 |
| 50 | 200 |

Assuming we wanted to know the transactions per second that could be expected with a user load of 30 users, we could construct the following graph:

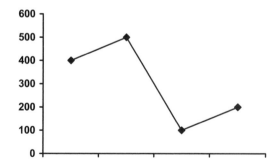

From this simple curve graphic, we can interpolate that the transaction per second rate of the database with a load of 30 users will probably be around 300 tps.

While interpolation helps you find where a data point falls within a set of known values, you can similarly use extrapolation to find where a data point falls outside of the known values. Here is a very simple example of extrapolation. We have a set of values:

| User Load | Trans/Sec |
|-----------|-----------|
| 10        | 50        |
| 20        | 100       |
| 30        | 150       |
| 40        | 200       |

Assuming we wanted to know the transactions per second that we could expect with a user load of 50 users, we could construct the following graph:

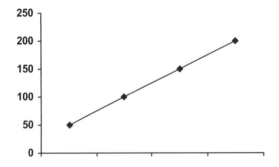

It is fairly simple, in this case, to extrapolate that since our values increased linearly, a user load of 50 would generate about 250 tps.

Interpolation and extrapolation can provide additional useful values to your benchmark report and can strongly contribute to the analysis and decision making made possible with the benchmark tests.

## Documenting the Final Analysis

Even when casually benchmarking various key differentiators, you should plan on delivering a document of your findings. As you prepare to create the benchmark findings, keep in mind the guidelines established for the scientific community when publishing the findings on important experiments. You should test...

- ... without bias or prejudice

- ... with clearly defined assumptions

- ... with a clearly-stated objective

- ... with an easily reproducible test case or benchmark

- ... while measuring and recording metrics accurately

- ... on relevant key differentiators

- ... using correct logical/statistical inference

- ... using proper attribution to sources or external references

By approaching benchmarking tests with these guidelines, you can easily deliver a benchmark report that is concise and based on clear and quantitative data. This is an ideal deliverable because benchmarking is almost always undertaken to improve decision making capabilities. Thus, your benchmark report will be a major factor influencing such things as a major new hardware or software purchase, plans for deploying a new product, timelines for important upgrades, and so forth.

Your benchmark report should include the following details:

- Preamble material, such as the date of the test and the names and roles of the testers.

- Configuration details:

    - The exact configuration of the hardware.

    - Information about the OS.

    - A full description of the database platform, its configuration settings, and operating environment (e.g. transaction isolation level).

- The objectives of the benchmark.

- The key differentiators.

- Full details about how the test was conducted.

- The test results throughout the timeline of the test.

- OS and database performance metrics correlated to the timeline of the test. Remember that a picture is worth a thousand words. So stick with graphics rather than tables to detail the performance metrics.

- An analysis of the benchmarking tests, including not only a major recommendation but also any informative or interesting side notes.

By following this general template, you will deliver a highly usable and informative benchmarking report.

## Conclusion

In this section, we have looked at the step in the benchmarking process where we collect, analyze, and assess the meaning of the results of our benchmarks. We have shown how to use Quest Software's Benchmark Factory to pull reports, for tests against both Oracle and Microsoft SQL Server and to collect performance metrics. This chapter has shown how to use Benchmark Factory to reveal high-level performance metrics that are immediately valuable, as well as how to create low-level reports that correlate the consumption of OS-level resources like CPU and memory to specific activities occurring during the benchmarks.

During the testing process, performance was monitored using Spotlight on SQL Server and Oracle to identify any problems. We gave a brief overview of how to use extrapolation and interpolation to calculate missing values. And finally we discussed how to document the benchmark results for maximum impact when the results are used to inform good decision making.

# Index

# About the Authors

***Dr. Bert Scalzo*** is one of the world's most highly-respected Oracle professionals with a breadth of experience spanning from Oracle 4 through Oracle 10g.

A former Oracle employee (Oracle Education and Consulting). Dr. Scalzo holds several Oracle Masters degrees, including a BS, MS and PhD in Computer Science and a Master Degree in Business Administration (MBA).

Dr. Scalzo is very active in the database community and he has written landmark articles for Oracle Technology Network (OTN), Oracle Informant, PC Week, Linux Journal, Oracle Magazine and www.linux.com.

Dr Scalzo is also the author of many database books, including TOAD Handbook, Toad Pocket Reference for Oracle (Pocket Reference (O'Reilly) and Oracle DBA Guide to Data Warehousing and Star Schemas.

Dr. Scalzo's key areas of DBA interest include Linux and data warehousing (he designed 7-Eleven Corporation's multi-terabyte, star-schema data warehouse). He also has written Oracle DBA Guide to Data Warehousing and Star Schemas. Dr. Scalzo is a product architect for Quest Software and a member of the Toad development team. He designed many of the features in the Toad for Oracle DBA module.

**Kevin Kline** is the director of technology for SQL Server Solutions at Quest Software and president of the international Professional Association for SQL Server (PASS) and frequently contributes to database technology magazines, Web sites, and discussion forums. Kevin is the author of "SQL in a Nutshell" (O'Reilly & Associates), "Transact-SQL Programming," and several other books about database technologies.

With more than eighteen years of experience in the IT industry, Kevin has worked on large-scale database projects at Deloitte & Touche, NASA and the US Army. In addition to being a Microsoft SQL Server MVP, Kevin is a top-rated speaker, appearing at international conferences including Microsoft TechEd, DevTeach, PASS, Microsoft IT Forum, and SQL Server Magazine Connections.

**Claudia Fernandez** is a Product Manager of Oracle development and Database Performance products at Quest Software. Claudia has contributed to the strategic direction of SQL tuning products for multiple RDBMS since early 2000 and has more than 10 years of industry experience working with RDBMS and related technologies.

Claudia holds a MS in Computer Science and has presented at several technical conferences on RDBMS and Application Performance Tuning topics. Prior to joining Quest she was the

Product Director and Tech Services Manager at Leccotech, a company specialized in SQL Tuning products acquired by Quest on 2004. Prior to LECCOTECH Ms. Fernandez worked as a Project Manager leading the development of several OLTP, DSS and Data Warehousing application projects. She started her career in the software and database industry as a developer of J2EE and database applications.

***Donald K. Burleson*** is one of the world's top Oracle Database experts with more than 20 years of full-time DBA experience.

He specializes in creating database architectures for very large online databases and he has worked with some of the world's most powerful and complex systems. A former Adjunct Professor, Don Burleson has written 34 books, and published more than 100 articles in National Magazines.

***Mike Ault*** is an Oracle Technical Specialist at Quest Software, and one of the leading names in Oracle technology. The author of more than 20 Oracle books and hundreds of articles in national publications, Mike Ault has five Oracle Masters Certificates and was the first popular Oracle author with his landmark book "Oracle7 Administration and Management". Mike also wrote several of the "Exam Cram" books, and enjoys a reputation as a leading author and Oracle consultant.

# About Mike Reed

When he first started drawing, Mike Reed drew just to amuse himself. It wasn't long though, before he knew he wanted to be an artist. Today he does illustrations for children's books, magazines, catalogs, and ads.

He also teaches illustration at the College of Visual Art in St. Paul, Minnesota. Mike Reed says, "Making pictures is like acting — you can paint yourself into the action." He often paints on the computer, but he also draws in pen and ink and paints in acrylics. He feels that learning to draw well is the key to being a successful artist.

Mike is regarded as one of the nation's premier illustrators and is the creator of the popular "Flame Warriors" illustrations at www.flamewarriors.com, a website devoted to Internet insults. "To enter his Flame Warriors site is sort of like entering a hellish Sesame Street populated by Oscar the Grouch and 83 of his relatives." – Los Angeles Times.
(http://redwing.hutman.net/%7Emreed/warriorshtm/lat.htm)

Mike Reed has always enjoyed reading. As a young child, he liked the Dr. Seuss books. Later, he started reading biographies and war stories. One reason why he feels lucky to be an illustrator is because he can listen to books on tape while he works. Mike is available to provide custom illustrations for all manner of publications at reasonable prices. Mike can be reached at www.mikereedillustration.com